The Working Alliance in Rational Emotive Behaviour Therapy

The Working Alliance in Rational Emotive Behaviour Therapy explores the principles and practice of REBT from the perspective of working alliance theory.

Windy Dryden seeks to debunk the myth that REBT neglects the therapeutic relationship by breaking down working alliance theory into specific domains in order to highlight its potential in this form of therapy. He introduces the reader to the *ABCs* of REBT and its basic practice, followed by the working alliance concept that forms the basis of this book. He then shows how the practice of REBT can be enhanced by the therapist attending to each of the four components of the alliance: bonds, views, goals and tasks.

The book is written for trainees and established therapists within REBT.

Windy Dryden PhD is Emeritus Professor of Psychotherapeutic Studies at Goldsmiths University of London and is an international authority on Rational Emotive Behaviour Therapy (REBT). He has worked in psychotherapy for over 45 years and is the author and editor of over 240 books.

Routledge Focus on Mental Health

Routledge Focus on Mental Health presents short books on current topics, linking in with cutting-edge research and practice.

For a full list of titles in this series, please visit www.routledge.com/ Routledge-Focus-on-Mental-Health/book-series/RFMH

The Working Alliance in Rational Emotive Behaviour Therapy
Principles and Practice

Windy Dryden

Routledge
Taylor & Francis Group

LONDON AND NEW YORK

First published 2021
by Routledge
2 Park Square, Milton Park, Abingdon, Oxon OX14 4RN

and by Routledge
605 Third Avenue, New York, NY 10158

Routledge is an imprint of the Taylor & Francis Group, an informa business

© 2021 Windy Dryden

The right of Windy Dryden to be identified as author of this work has been asserted by him in accordance with sections 77 and 78 of the Copyright, Designs and Patents Act 1988.

British Library Cataloguing-in-Publication Data
A catalogue record for this book is available from the British Library

Library of Congress Cataloging-in-Publication Data
A catalog record has been requested for this book

ISBN: 978-1-032-05025-6 (hbk)
ISBN: 978-1-032-05026-3 (pbk)
ISBN: 978-1-003-19569-6 (ebk)

Typeset in Times New Roman
by Newgen Publishing UK

The Working Alliance in Rational Emotive Behaviour Therapy
Principles and Practice

Windy Dryden

Routledge
Taylor & Francis Group

LONDON AND NEW YORK

First published 2021
by Routledge
2 Park Square, Milton Park, Abingdon, Oxon OX14 4RN

and by Routledge
605 Third Avenue, New York, NY 10158

Routledge is an imprint of the Taylor & Francis Group, an informa business

© 2021 Windy Dryden

British Library Cataloguing-in-Publication Data
A catalogue record for this book is available from the British Library

Library of Congress Cataloging-in-Publication Data
A catalog record has been requested for this book

ISBN: 978-1-032-05025-6 (hbk)
ISBN: 978-1-032-05026-3 (pbk)
ISBN: 978-1-003-19569-6 (ebk)

Typeset in Times New Roman
by Newgen Publishing UK

Contents

Introduction

In this book, I will consider the principles and practice of Rational Emotive Behaviour Therapy (REBT) from the perspective of working alliance theory (Bordin, 1979). The first two chapters are introductory chapters. Chapter 1 introduces you, the reader, to the *ABCs* of REBT and its basic practice, while Chapter 2 introduces you to the working alliance concept that forms the basis of this book. In Chapters 3–6, I discuss how the practice of REBT can be enhanced by the therapist attending to each of the four components of the alliance: bonds, views, goals and tasks.

Let me be clear about what I have set out to do in this book and what I have not set out to do. My basic aim is primarily to help REB therapists improve their practice of REBT by attending to general factors that do not sit centre stage in other REBT books and manuals. My position is that REB therapists can increase their effectiveness by a) forming and maintaining effective bonds with their clients, b) ensuring that they have shared views of salient aspects of the REBT process, c) negotiating shared goals which help clients to gain what they want to from the process and d) encouraging their clients and themselves to use the most suitable tasks in the service of these goals.

There is an immense amount of research on the working alliance and on its ruptures and repair and it is not my intention to review this work in the book, a task that would necessitate a far longer text and also detract from the basic message of the book. This is that REB therapists can become better therapists not only by becoming more technically efficient in REBT techniques but also by better managing the nuances of the working alliance between themselves and their clients.

Windy Dryden
London and Eastbourne

1   The *ABCs* of REBT

Rational Emotive Behaviour Therapy (REBT) is an approach to therapy that can be placed firmly in the cognitive-behavioural tradition of psychotherapy, meaning that it mainly focuses on the way that we think and behave when understanding our emotional responses. REBT was founded in 1955 by Dr Albert Ellis, an American clinical psychologist who brought together his interests in philosophy and psychology which are still present in this approach over 65 years on. One of the hallmarks of REBT is that it holds that people can be taught and can learn the principles of good mental health.

In this opening chapter, I will introduce REBT to those who are not familiar with it and will do so by outlining REBT's views about psychological disturbance and health. I will do this by presenting my situational version of REBT's *ABC* model that Albert Ellis first introduced over 65 years ago.[1] Before I present my situational *ABC* model, let me summarise its main features:

- It roots the *ABC* components in a specific situational context, thus underscoring that a client tends to disturb themself most in specific situational contexts.
- It puts forward the view that the *A* that triggers *B* is best described as an adversity.
- It thus distinguishes between an adversity and the situation in which the adversity occurs.
- It makes clear that *Cs* can be emotional, behavioural and cognitive.
- It is very explicit in differentiating rigid and extreme basic attitudes from flexible and non-extreme attitudes by making clear the different components of each.

---

1 There have been many versions of the *ABC* model (e.g. Grieger & Boyd, 1980; Walen, DiGiuseppe & Dryden, 1992; Wessler & Wessler, 1980; Woods, 1991).

I will briefly describe the model before discussing each element in greater detail.

'Situation'
A client does not react in a vacuum. Rather, they think, feel and act in specific situations. The term 'situation' in the ABC model refers to a descriptive account of the event and its context in which the client responded emotionally, behaviourally and cognitively.

A = Adversity
Within this specific situation, when a client has a significant emotional reaction, it is usually to a key aspect of this situation. This is known as the adversity.

B = Basic attitude[2]
It is a major premise of REBT that while a client's emotions are usually about an adversity, this A does not cause their emotional reaction. Rather, the client's emotions are primarily determined by the basic attitudes that they hold towards the adversity.

C = Consequences
These are the consequences of the client holding a set of basic attitudes at B towards the adversity at A. There are three such consequences: emotional, behavioural and thinking. Thus, when a client holds an attitude towards an adversity, they will tend to experience an emotion, and a tendency to act and think in specific ways.
    Let me now discuss each of these elements in greater detail.

'Situation'

As I said earlier, emotional episodes do not take place in a vacuum. Instead, they occur in specific 'situations'. Such 'situations' are viewed in the 'situational ABC' model as descriptions of actual events about which the client forms inferences (see below). 'Situations' exist in time. Thus, they may occur in the past (e.g. 'My boss asked me to see her at the end of the day'), in the present (e.g. 'My boss is asking me to see her at the end of the day') or in the future (e.g. 'My boss will ask me to see her at the end of the day'). When a 'situation' occurs in the future, we cannot say that it will happen, but in REBT we encourage the client to assume that it will occur. Note that each of the situations

---

2 The term 'basic attitude' is used here to preserve the B in the ABC framework. It refers to a person's attitude towards adversity which lies at the 'base' of their emotional, behavioural and thinking responses towards the adversity, as will be presently shown.

listed is a description and does not contain inferential meaning (see below).

'Situations' may refer to internal events (i.e. events that occur within ourselves, e.g. thoughts, feelings, bodily sensations, aches and pains, etc.) or to external events (i.e. events that occur outside ourselves, e.g. the client's boss asking to see them). Their defining characteristic is as stated before: they are descriptions of events and do not include inferential meaning.

A

As I said above, *A* stands for an adversity. This is the aspect of the 'situation' about which the client experiences an emotional reaction. Let me make several points about *A*.

1. *An A is usually an inference and needs to be differentiated from the 'situation' about which it is made.*

    An inference is an interpretation or hunch about the 'situation', whereas the 'situation' is purely descriptive. Let me provide a clinical example to make this distinction clear.

    Imagine that a client receives a message from their boss to the effect that the boss wants to see them at the end of the day. The client thinks this means that they are in trouble. The 'situation' is: 'My boss wants to see me at the end of the day', while the client's adversity (*A*) is: 'I am in trouble'. As can be seen from this example, the 'situation' is a description of the facts of the matter, whereas the *A* is the key inference that the client has made about the 'situation'. It is key because it is the aspect of the situation to which the client has an emotional response. When a client has a significant emotional response to a 'situation', the *A* represents the personalised inferential meaning that the client gives to the 'situation'. As I said earlier, I refer to the *A* as an adversity.

2. *Inferences that usually comprise the A can be true or false, and, as such, when the client makes an inference, they need to evaluate it against the available evidence.*

    In the above example, it may be true that the client is in trouble when they go to see their boss at the end of the working day, or it may be false. All the client can do is to consider the available evidence and come up with their 'best bet' about what is going to happen at the meeting with the boss. This involves the client considering such factors as a) what has happened in the past when their boss has asked to see them, b) what the client has done that may have led to them getting into trouble with their boss, and c) how critical or otherwise the boss is in general.

In REBT, we suggest that the client asks themself these questions when they are not in a disturbed frame of mind. Consequently, the therapist invites the client to assume temporarily that their *A* is true, that they are in trouble when they go to see their boss. In doing so, the therapist helps the client to deal with this adversity in as healthily a manner as possible.

3. *An A can be about a past, present or future event.*
   When the client has an *A* about a past, present or future 'situation', they give that event inferential meaning. Thus:
   - Past 'situation' = My boyfriend did not return my call.
   - *A* about past 'situation' = My boyfriend does not care for me.
   - Present 'situation' = My father is discussing the value of saving regularly.
   - *A* about present 'situation' = My father is criticising me for overspending.
   - Future 'situation' = The hospital will contact me with the results of my blood test.
   - *A* about future 'situation' = The blood test will show that I am severely ill.

4. *An A can be about a situation external to the client or a situation internal to the client.*
   The defining characteristic of this *A* is again its inferential nature. For example:
   - External 'situation' = Letter with a cheque in it has gone missing.
   - *A* about external 'situation' = Somebody has stolen my cheque.
   - Internal 'situation' = I have just had a thought about me hitting someone.
   - *A* about internal 'situation' = I am losing control.

B

The *ABC* model of psychological disturbance states that people disturb themselves at *C* about adversities at *A* because they hold a set of rigid and extreme basic attitudes at *B* towards these adversities. For them to respond healthily to these adversities, they will need to hold a set of flexible and non-extreme attitudes towards them.

These basic attitudes can be rigid and extreme (or unhealthy) or flexible and non-extreme attitudes (or healthy). A client can hold basic attitudes towards descriptive 'situations', but more often they will hold basic attitudes towards the main adversity that features in their emotional problem. I will discuss healthy basic attitudes first.

Healthy basic attitudes

REBT argues that there are four healthy basic attitudes which have the following five major characteristics:

* flexible or non-extreme
* conducive to mental health
* helpful to the client as they strive towards their goals
* true
* logical.

Now let me discuss the four healthy basic attitudes put forward by REBT theory:

* flexible attitude
* non-awfulising attitude
* bearability attitude
* unconditional acceptance attitude.

REBT theory holds that the flexible attitude is primary in accounting for a psychologically healthy response to an adversity and the other three attitudes, which are known as non-extreme attitudes, are derived from the primary flexible attitude.

Flexible attitude

A flexible attitude has two components. The first component is called the 'desire' component. Here, the client acknowledges what they want. The second component is called the 'negated demand' component. Here, the client acknowledges that they do not have to get what they want.

In short, we have:

flexible attitude = 'desire' component + 'negated demand' component

Non-awfulising attitude

A non-awfulising attitude has two components. The first component is the 'evaluation of badness' component. Here, the client acknowledges that it is bad not getting what they want. The second component is called the 'non-awfulising' component. Here, the client acknowledges that while it is bad not getting what they want, it is not awful, terrible or the end of the world.

In short, we have:

non-awfulising attitude = 'evaluation of badness' component +
'non-awfulising' component

Bearability attitude

A bearability attitude has five components. The first component may be
called the 'struggle' component because the client recognises that it is a
struggle to bear not getting what they want. The second component is
called the 'bearability' component. Here, the client acknowledges that
while it is a struggle to bear not getting what they want, they can bear
it. The third component is called the 'worth bearing' component and
points to the fact that not only can the client bear not getting what they
want, but it is also worth it to them to bear it. The fourth component is
called the 'willingness' component. Here, the client indicates that they
are willing to bear not getting what they want. The fifth component is
called the 'going to' component. Here, the client indicates that not only
are they willing to bear not getting what they want, but they are also
going to do so.
    In short, we have:

bearability attitude = 'struggle' component +
'bearability' component + 'worth bearing' component +
'willingness' component + 'going to' component

Unconditional acceptance attitude

There are three types of unconditional acceptance attitude: an unconditional self-acceptance attitude where the client accepts themself
unconditionally for not meeting their own desires, an unconditional
other-acceptance attitude where the client accepts another person or
other people unconditionally for not meeting their desires, and an
unconditional acceptance of life conditions attitude where the client
accepts life conditions unconditionally when these conditions don't
meet their desires.
    There are three components to an unconditional acceptance atti-
tude, which I will illustrate with reference to an unconditional self-
acceptance attitude. The first component is called the 'negatively
evaluated aspect' component. Here, the client recognises that their
behaviour has led them to not meeting their desires, and they evaluate
this particular aspect negatively. The second component is called

the 'negated global negative evaluation' component. Here, the client acknowledges that while they have acted badly, the whole of them is not bad. The third component is called the 'asserted complex fallible' component. Whereas in the second component, the client negates the view that they are a bad person, for example, here they assert what they are: a complex, fallible human being.

In short, we have:

> unconditional acceptance attitude = 'negatively evaluated aspect' component + 'negated global negative evaluation' component + 'asserted complex fallible' component

Unhealthy basic attitudes

REBT argues that there are four unhealthy basic attitudes which have the following five major characteristics:

- rigid or extreme
- conducive to psychological disturbance
- unhelpful to the client as they strive towards their goals
- false
- illogical.

Now let me discuss the four unhealthy basic attitudes put forward by REBT theory:

- rigid attitude
- awfulising attitude
- unbearability attitude
- devaluation attitude.

REBT theory holds that the rigid attitude is primary in accounting for psychologically disturbed responses to adversities and the other three attitudes, which are known as extreme attitudes, are derived from the primary rigid attitude.

Rigid attitude

A rigid attitude has two components. The first component is called the 'desire' component and is the same as the desire component of a flexible attitude. Again, the client acknowledges what they want. The second component is called the 'demand' component. Here, the client acknowledges what they want and demands they have to get what they want.

In short, we have:

rigid attitude = 'desire' component + 'demand' component

Awfulising attitude

An awfulising attitude has two components. The first component is the 'evaluation of badness' component and is the same as the 'evaluation of badness' component of a non-awfulising attitude. The second component is called the 'awfulising' component. Here, the client acknowledges that it is bad not getting what they want, but they then transform this non-extreme evaluation of badness into an extreme evaluation of awful, terrible or the end of the world.

In short, we have:

awfulising attitude = 'evaluation of badness' component + 'awfulising' component

Unbearability attitude

An unbearability attitude has two components. The first component is the 'struggle' component and is the same as the 'struggle' component of a bearability attitude. The second component is called the 'unbearability' component. Here, the client acknowledges that it is a struggle not getting what they want and then they transform this non-extreme component of struggle into an extreme component of not being able to bear the struggle.

In short, we have:

unbearability attitude = 'struggle' component + 'unbearability' component

Devaluation attitude

There are three types of devaluation attitude: a self-devaluation attitude where the client devalues themself for not meeting their demands, an other-devaluation attitude where the client devalues another person or other people for not meeting their demands, and a devaluation of life conditions attitude where the client devalues life conditions when they don't meet their demands.

A devaluation attitude has two components. The first component is the 'negatively evaluated aspect' component and is the same as the 'negatively evaluated aspect' component of the unconditional acceptance attitude. The second component is called the 'asserted global negative evaluation' component. Here the client gives themself a global negative rating for not meeting their demands, for example.

In short, we have:

devaluation attitude = 'negatively evaluated aspect' component + 'asserted global negative evaluation' component

Table 1.1 summarises the shared and differentiating components of flexible/non-extreme attitudes and rigid/extreme attitudes and Table 1.2 provides examples of both attitudes and components.

C

C stands for the consequences that a client experiences when they hold a basic attitude at *B* towards the adversity at *A*. There are three major consequences which I will consider separately, but which, in reality, occur together: emotional *Cs*, behavioural *Cs* and thinking *Cs*.

Emotional Cs

When the client holds a set of flexible and non-extreme attitudes towards an adversity, their emotional *C* will be negative but healthy. Yes, that is correct; negative emotions can be healthy. Thus, when a client infers that they are facing a threat, it is healthy for them to feel concerned, and if they have experienced a loss, it is healthy for them to feel sad. Other healthy negative emotions (so called because they feel unpleasant but help the client deal constructively with adversities) are: remorse, disappointment, sorrow, healthy anger, healthy jealousy and healthy envy.

When the client holds a set of rigid and extreme attitudes towards the same adversity, their emotional *C* will be negative and unhealthy. Thus, when a client again infers that they are facing a threat, it is unhealthy for them to feel anxious and, again, if they have experienced a loss, it is unhealthy for them to feel depressed. Other unhealthy negative emotions (so called because they feel unpleasant and they interfere with the client dealing constructively with adversities) are: guilt, shame, hurt, unhealthy anger, unhealthy jealousy and unhealthy envy.

Table 1.1 Flexible/non-extreme attitudes vs rigid/extreme attitudes: shared and differentiating components

Attitude	Shared Component	Differentiating Components
Flexible attitude	'Desire' component	'Negated demand' component
Rigid attitude	'Desire' component	'Demand' component
Non-awfulising attitude	'Evaluation of badness' component	'Non-awfulising' component
Awfulising attitude	'Evaluation of badness' component	'Awfulising' component
Bearability attitude	'Struggle' component	'Bearability' component, 'Worth bearing' component, 'Willingness' component, 'Going to' component
Unbearability attitude	'Struggle' component	'Unbearability component
Unconditional acceptance attitude	'Negatively evaluated aspect' component	'Negated global negative evaluation' component, 'Asserted complex fallible' component
Devaluation attitude	'Negatively evaluated aspect' component	'Asserted global negative evaluation' component

Table 1.2 **Flexible/non-extreme attitudes vs rigid/extreme attitudes: examples with shared and differentiating components**

Attitude	*Shared Component*	*Differentiating Components*
I want to do well, but I don't have to do so **Flexible attitude**	*I want to do well...* **('Desire' component)**	*...but I don't have to do so* **('Negated demand' component)**
I want to well and therefore I have to do so **Rigid attitude**		*...and therefore I have to do so* **('Demand' component)**
It's bad if I don't do well, but it is not terrible **Non-awfulising attitude**	*It's bad if I don't do well...* **('Evaluation of badness' component)**	*...but it is not terrible* **('Non-awfulising' component)**
It's bad if I don't do well and therefore it's terrible **Awfulising attitude**		*...and therefore it's terrible* **('Awfulising' component)**

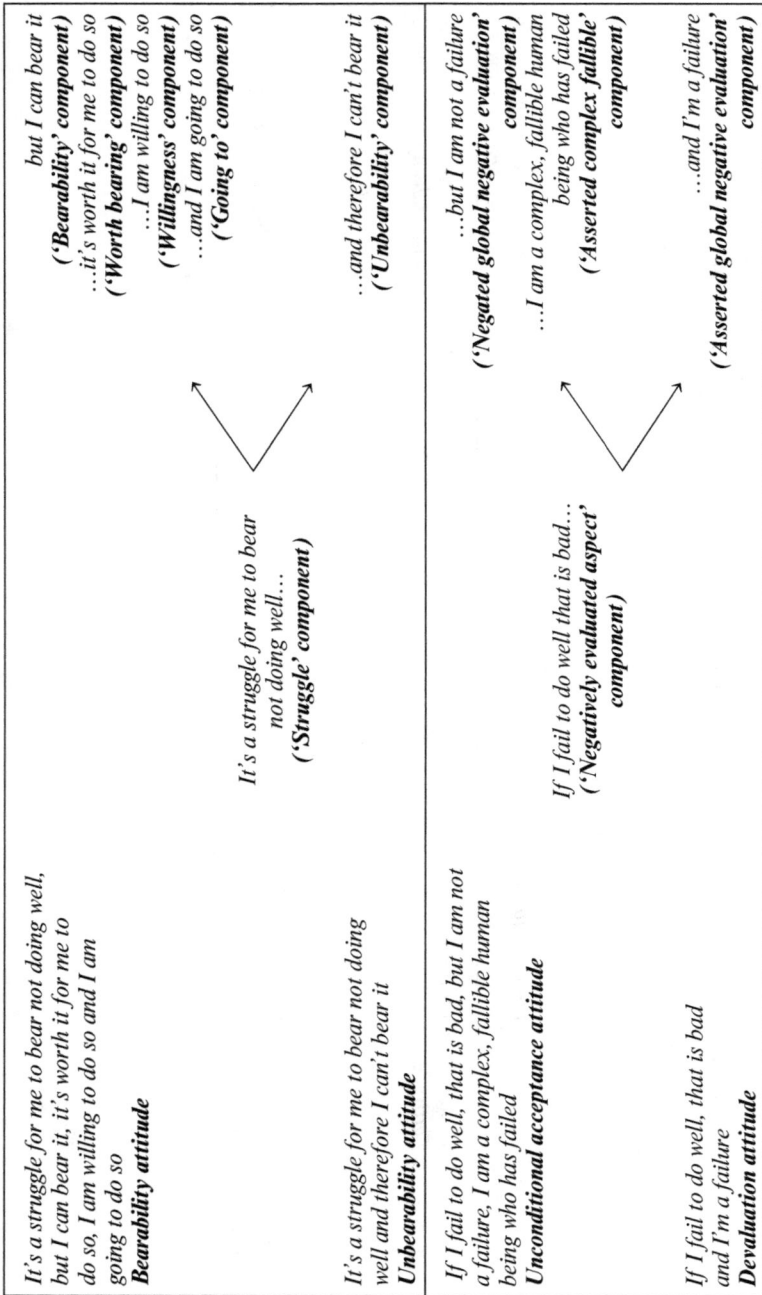

It's a struggle for me to bear not doing well, but I can bear it, it's worth it for me to do so, I am willing to do so and I am going to do so
Bearability attitude

It's a struggle for me to bear not doing well and therefore I can't bear it
Unbearability attitude

It's a struggle for me to bear not doing well...
('Struggle' component)

but I can bear it
('Bearability' component)
...it's worth it for me to do so
('Worth bearing' component)
...I am willing to do so
('Willingness' component)
...and I am going to do so
('Going to' component)

...and therefore I can't bear it
('Unbearability' component)

If I fail to do well, that is bad, but I am not a failure, I am a complex, fallible human being who has failed
Unconditional acceptance attitude

If I fail to do well, that is bad and I'm a failure
Devaluation attitude

If I fail to do well that is bad...
('Negatively evaluated aspect' component)

...but I am not a failure
('Negated global negative evaluation' component)
...I am a complex, fallible human being who has failed
('Asserted complex fallible' component)

...and I'm a failure
('Asserted global negative evaluation' component)

Behavioural Cs

When the client holds a set of flexible and non-extreme attitudes towards an adversity, their behavioural *C* is likely to be constructive. Such behaviour is constructive in three ways. First, it will help the client to change the adversity that they are facing if it can be changed. Second, it will help them to make a healthy adjustment if the adversity cannot be changed and, third, it will help them to go forward and make progress at achieving their goals.

When the client holds a set of rigid and extreme attitudes towards the adversity, their behavioural *C* is likely to be unconstructive. Such behaviour is unconstructive in three ways. First, it will not help the client to change the adversity that they are facing if it can be changed. Indeed, such unconstructive behaviour will often make a bad situation worse. Second, it will prevent the client from making a healthy adjustment if the adversity cannot be changed and, third, it will take them away from pursuing their goals.

Thinking Cs

When the client holds a set of flexible and non-extreme attitudes towards an adversity, their subsequent thinking (or thinking *C*) is likely to be constructive. Such thinking is constructive in three ways. First, it is realistic and allows the client to deal with probable outcomes. Second, it is balanced and recognises, for example, that the client will get a range of positive, neutral and negative responses to their behaviour. As a result, these thinking *Cs* enable the client to respond constructively to realistically perceived situations. Third, the client's thinking is likely to be problem-solving and non-ruminative in nature.

When the client holds a set of rigid and extreme attitudes towards the adversity, their subsequent thinking (or thinking *C*) is likely to be unconstructive. Such thinking is unconstructive in three ways. First, it is unrealistic in that the client will tend to think that low probability, highly aversive outcomes are likely to happen. Second, it is skewed in that the client thinks, for example, that most people will respond to them negatively, a few may respond to them neutrally, but nobody will respond to them positively. As a result, these thinking *Cs* interfere with the client's ability to respond constructively to realistically perceived situations. Third, the client's thinking is likely to be ruminative in nature.

I have summarised REBT's 'situational *ABC*' models of psychological disturbance and health in Tables 1.3 and 1.4 respectively.

Table 1.3 'Situational *ABC* model of psychological health

'Situation' = Objectively described event

A = **Adversity** (the aspect of the situation to which the client responds emotionally, behaviourally and cognitively)

B = **Healthy basic attitudes:**   Flexible attitude
Non-awfulising attitude
Bearability attitude
Unconditional acceptance attitude

C = **Consequences**
Emotional (healthy negative)
Behavioural (constructive)
Thinking (realistic, balanced and non-ruminative)

Table 1.4 'Situational *ABC* model of psychological disturbance

---

'Situation' = Objectively described event

A = **Adversity** (the aspect of the situation to which the client responds emotionally, behaviourally and cognitively)

B = **Unhealthy basic attitudes**:   Rigid attitude
Awfulising attitude
Unbearability attitude
Devaluation attitude

C = **Consequences**
Emotional (unhealthy negative)
Behavioural (unconstructive)
Thinking (unrealistic, skewed and ruminative)

REBT practice

What I have discussed so far has outlined the model of psychological disturbance and health that REB therapists use to inform their understanding of their clients' problems and what would constitute healthy solutions to these problems. While the rest of this book will consider the practice of REBT from a working alliance perspective, it would be useful if I gave an outline of the process of REBT practice, particularly for those who are new to REBT.

Induction and informed consent

As in other therapies, the REB therapist will elicit the client's informed consent to proceed before embarking on therapy. This involves the therapist making clear such practical matters as their policy of confidentiality, cancellation of sessions and fee issues. However, it is also vital that the therapist outlines the nature of REBT for the client and what it expects of them both. If the client understands and agrees with these points, then they are deemed to have given their informed consent, which may be confirmed verbally or in writing. I will discuss these matters more fully in Chapter 4.

Problem assessment

After the client has indicated why they are seeking therapy, has told the therapist what they think it is crucial for the therapist to know about themself, their past and the context of their problem, and the therapist has had an opportunity to respond empathically to what the client has said (see Chapter 3), the therapist gets down to the business of assessing and dealing with the client's problems one at a time. Here the REB therapist will use the *ABC* of psychological disturbance that I described earlier in this chapter (see also Chapter 4).

Problem-related goal-setting

During the assessment process, it is also vital for the therapist to help the client to set goals that relate directly to the client's problems as assessed. In doing this, the REB therapist will use the *ABC* of psychological health that I described earlier in this chapter (see also Chapter 5).

Attitude change I: promoting intellectual insight

It follows from what I have said in this chapter that the prime task of the REB therapist is to help the client to change their set of rigid and extreme attitudes to an alternative set of flexible and non-extreme attitudes. Ellis (1963) made a useful distinction between intellectual insight and emotional insight that is useful here. In this context, when a client has intellectual insight into their flexible and non-extreme attitudes, they understand that these attitudes are healthier for them than their rigid and extreme attitudes, but such insight has not yet influenced the way they feel, act and think towards the adversities that feature in their problems. Helping the client achieve intellectual insight is an important stage (and one that I will discuss in Chapter 4), but one that is insufficient for significant change to occur in REBT.

Attitude change II: promoting emotional insight

For such significant change to occur in REBT, the client would need to achieve emotional insight which, in this context, means that the client has a deep conviction which impacts healthily on the way they feel, act and think towards the adversities that feature in their problems to the point that they have solved the problems. I discuss this also in Chapter 4.

Relapse prevention

Once the client has solved their problems, they need help to maintain these gains, and this involves the therapist doing some relapse prevention with them. In doing this, the therapist helps them to identify and deal with vulnerability factors and the inevitable lapses that they will experience. I discuss this issue in Chapter 6.

Encouraging clients to be their own therapists

Ideally, the therapist will want to encourage the client to assume increasing responsibility for their therapy over the course of the therapeutic process to the extent that they will be able to become their own REB therapists. However, as I discuss in Chapter 6, not all clients are interested in doing this.

In the following chapter, I will present and briefly discuss the working alliance framework, which forms the foundation of this book, before considering its four components separately in Chapters 3–6.

2 The working alliance in psychotherapy
An introduction

The professional psychotherapy literature has often given the impression that Rational Emotive Behaviour Therapy is a technical approach to psychotherapy. For example, it has tended to emphasise therapist activities such as:

- accurately assessing clients' problems with reference to REBT's ABC model of unhealthy responses (C) to life's adversities (A)
- helping clients to set problem-related goals with reference to REBT's ABC model of healthy responses (C) to life's adversities (A)
- disputing clients' rigid and extreme basic attitudes (B) that are considered to be chiefly responsible for clients' unhealthy responses towards A
- helping clients to construct and rehearse an alternative set of flexible and non-extreme basic attitudes at B so that they can respond healthily to A, and then either to change A if it can be changed or to adjust constructively to A if it cannot be changed.

The REB therapist does certainly need to be very confident and accomplished in the above areas. However, it should also be remembered that psychotherapy is essentially an interpersonal process – regardless of whether the therapist and client meet face-to-face or online. As such, the main message in this book is that effective REBT is practised within the context of an effective working alliance between the REB therapist and client. I will be discussing the working alliance with reference to an expanded version of the framework initially put forward by Ed Bordin (1979). Bordin proposed that the working alliance is comprised of three overlapping domains: bonds, goals and tasks. My own opinion is that this tri-partite model of the working alliance leaves out a fourth important domain which I have called 'views' and incorporated in my expanded version of Bordin's original model (Dryden, 2006, 2011) – see Figure 2.1.

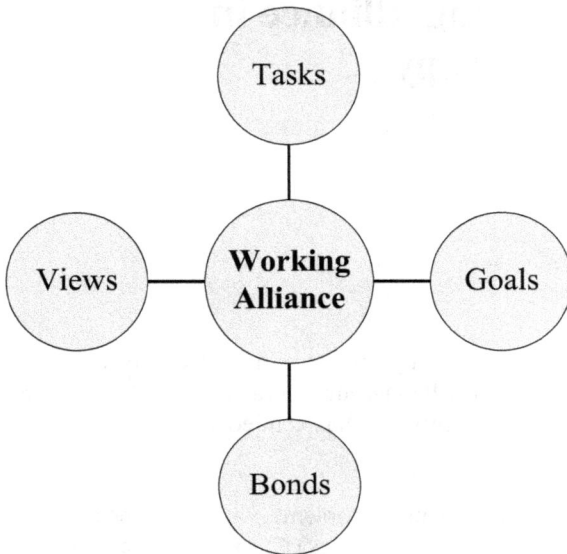

Figure 2.1 **The working alliance diagram (Dryden, 2011)**

In the rest of this chapter, I will provide a brief overview of this expanded version of the working alliance. I will then discuss in the following chapters how each component of the working alliance can inform REBT practice.

Bonds

The bonds domain of the working alliance refers to the interpersonal connectedness between the therapist and client, with respect to the following relational areas:

* the 'core conditions'
* the client's feelings of safety and trust in the therapist
* the therapist's interactive stance and style of doing therapy
* the therapist's influence base
* transference and countertransference.

The 'core conditions'

Carl Rogers, the founder of client-centred/person-centred therapy, wrote an influential article in 1957 entitled 'The necessary and sufficient conditions of therapeutic personality change'. In this article, Rogers (1957) put forward three therapist-related conditions that have become colloquially known as the 'core conditions'. According to Rogers, the presence of these conditions would result in the client achieving a measure of constructive therapeutic change. The first condition concerns the therapist being *congruent and integrated* in the relationship, as opposed to assuming a façade. This condition has latterly been referred to as 'genuineness'. The second condition refers to the therapist experiencing *unconditional positive regard*, also known as 'prizing', for the client. The third condition refers to the therapist experiencing *empathic understanding* of the client's experience 'as if' it was their own without losing this 'as if' quality.

Rogers (1957) made the point in his original paper that it was important for the client to experience the therapist's understanding and unconditional positive regard. While he did not make this point in relation to the therapist's genuineness, I think it also applies to this condition, given that if the client were to experience the therapist as adopting a façade or 'playing the role' of being a therapist, this would nullify the therapeutic potency of this 'core condition'. Person-centred therapists have later emphasised the point that it is this experiential component that makes the 'core conditions' therapeutic. To summarise, I would say that, from a person-centred perspective, the client will achieve a measure of constructive therapeutic change to the extent that they experience their therapist as genuine, prizing of them as a person, and understanding of their internal frame of reference.

The client's feelings of safety, trust and faith in the therapist

This area of the therapeutic bond concerns the feelings and attitudes that the client has towards their therapist. It is focused on the extent to which the client experiences a sense of trust in the therapist, the degree to which the client feels safe in the therapeutic relationship and the amount of faith the client has in their therapist's ability to help them.

Different approaches to therapy emphasise different ways in which the therapist can promote client safety, trust and faith and I will discuss REBT's stance on this issue in Chapter 3.

The therapist's interactive stance

This third area relevant to the therapeutic bond concerns the interactive stance of the therapist. Different therapeutic approaches recommend different interactive stances, which vary along two main dimensions. One of these dimensions concerns level of activity, and the other concerns level of direction. I will discuss REBT's position on interactive stances in Chapter 3.

The therapist's style of doing therapy

The therapist's interactive stance can be combined with different therapeutic styles. One aspect of therapeutic style is the degree to which the therapist adopts a formal or informal style of interaction with the client. Different schools of therapy can emphasise different styles. The degree of formality also has a bearing on the extent to which the therapist uses humour (or not) in their work with clients. Again, I will discuss REBT's position on such issues in the next chapter.

The influence base of the therapist

An alternative approach to considering the bond between the client and therapist emanated from social psychology in the 1980s (e.g. Dorn, 1984). Dorn encourages us to think about influence processes in the working alliance. While many may resist thinking about the therapeutic relationship in this way, it could be appropriate and useful to acknowledge the role of influence if one takes the view that the therapist is trying to encourage and persuade the client to live a more resourceful and psychologically healthy life. This perspective encourages us to consider, for example, whether the client is most likely to listen to, and be influenced by, their therapist if they like their therapist and/or if they are impressed by their therapist's level of expertise. Similarly, the therapist is advised to identify the client's influence preferences and make use of these where possible.

Transference and countertransference

The term 'transference' is used in therapy to refer to a situation in which the client redirects their feelings about a significant person in their life, typically a parent, towards their therapist. The therapist then employs these feelings to help the client to learn more about their conflicts. On the other hand, the term 'countertransference' is used in therapy to refer to a situation in which the therapist experiences feelings towards their client. This can happen in both situations when the therapist redirects their feelings for a significant person in their own life towards their client, and situations when the therapist can learn something valuable about what their client is attempting to elicit in them. I will discuss REBT's position on this issue in Chapter 3.

Views

The views domain of the working alliance points to the client's and therapist's understandings about important aspects of psychotherapy and, in particular, the following pertinent issues:

- the client's emotional problems, their nature and what accounts for them
- how the client's problems can be best addressed
- the practical aspects of therapy.

The client's emotional problem, its nature and what accounts for the problem

Working alliance theory does not specify what problem a client may have, the nature of this problem or what might account for the existence of the problem. Instead, it highlights the importance of therapists (whatever their therapeutic approach) and clients sharing a common understanding of these issues. If a client thinks they have a problem with anger, and their therapist understands that the problem is more anxiety-related, this is likely to undermine therapeutic progress. Likewise, if the therapist thinks that a client's symptoms are indicative of a psychological problem, while the client attributes them to a medical problem (this is a frequent disagreement with health anxiety), then therapeutic progress is likely to falter. In addition, if the therapist and client disagree on their understanding of what determines the client's problem and how it is being maintained, it is again difficult to see how the therapy could be effective.

How the client's problems can be best addressed

In the views domain, the importance of both therapist and client being in agreement about how the client is going to address their problem is emphasised. Otherwise, the client will 'resist' the therapist's suggested approaches to tackling the problem. Interestingly, the client may even reject evidence-based suggestions from their therapist, because they have a different view from that of the therapist about how to best tackle the problem. The therapist therefore needs to take extra care to take into account the client's views in order to make progress.

The practical aspects of therapy

The therapist and client need to agree on several practical matters before the client can give their informed consent to proceed, and in order to ensure a smooth therapeutic journey. Such practical matters include:

- the therapist's fees and when and how they are to be paid
- the therapist's cancellation policy
- the therapist's confidentiality policy
- the length of therapy
- the length of each therapy session
- the frequency of therapy sessions.

Some of the above practical matters may be subject to change as therapy evolves (e.g. the frequency of therapy sessions and length of therapy). Therefore, it is important for the therapist to have a way of keeping agreements on practical matters up to date.

To summarise this section about the views domain, working alliance theory holds that when a client and therapist share similar views on a range of therapeutic issues, then therapy is more likely to be effective than when their views differ. In situations where views differ, the differences need to be recognised, acknowledged and discussed in an open manner. Such discussion can take place in what I call the 'reflection process', which I will describe in the next chapter.

Goals

The goals domain of the working alliance directs attention to the therapist's and client's objectives for working together. Therefore goals could be considered to be the raison d'être of the therapeutic process. The issue of goals in therapy might initially seem to be relatively straightforward: the client is experiencing some kind of psychological distress, wants relief from this distress and wants more fulfilment in life; and the therapist's goal is to help the client to achieve their goals. However, the situation is often more complex than this, and there are several issues to bear in mind when goals become the main focus in therapy. I will discuss these in detail in Chapter 5, especially as they relate to the practice of REBT. For now I will make a couple of more general observations about goals.

Goals and the working alliance

From the perspective of working alliance theory, therapy is more likely to be effective if the therapist and client agree about where they are heading in relation to the client's goals for therapy and they agree to work towards these goals (e.g. Bordin, 1979). It is outcome goals that Bordin is essentially concerned with – that is, goals that reflect the client's desired outcomes at the conclusion of therapy. There are also other types of goals such as process goals and session goals. However, outcome goals are the most important goals. I will discuss this issue more fully in Chapter 5.

Different approaches, different stances on goals

Different approaches to therapy have different viewpoints on therapeutic goals:

- Some approaches value working with client goals, while others regard doing so as limiting.
- Some approaches argue that client goals should be set at the outset, while others argue that clients need a long period of exploration before engaging with the question of outcome goals.
- Some approaches are prepared to work with vague client goals, while others prefer to work with specific goals.

I will discuss REBT's position on goals in Chapter 5.

Tasks

The tasks domain of the working alliance points to the execution of tasks by both the therapist and the client that are intended to help the client. In this respect, it highlights several task-related issues that apply to any psychotherapeutic approach. I will list these issues here – under the headings of client tasks and therapist tasks – and will revisit this topic when I discuss tasks with specific reference to REBT in Chapter 6.

Client tasks

It is tempting for a client to think that all they have to do to be healed is to turn up at the therapist's consulting room. However, in all approaches to therapy there is some kind of expectation that the client will engage in therapeutic tasks. In this respect, it is important to consider the following questions:

- Does the client understand the nature of their therapeutic tasks? The more the client understands the nature of their therapeutic tasks and activities, the more they will engage with therapy.

- Does the client understand the instrumental value of their therapeutic tasks?

  It is very important, from a working alliance perspective, that clients understand the association between carrying out their therapeutic tasks and achieving their outcome goals.

- What is the relationship between salient client factors and the execution of their therapeutic tasks?

  There are a number of factors that I will mention here that I will expand upon in Chapter 6:

  - The client should have the ability to carry out their therapeutic tasks.
  - The client should have the skills to carry out their therapeutic tasks.
  - The client should have sufficient confidence to carry out their therapeutic tasks.
  - The client should understand the therapist's tasks.

Therapist tasks

All approaches to psychotherapy expect the therapist to implement a number of therapeutic tasks. While some of these tasks are common to all therapy approaches, other tasks are specific to particular approaches. I will discuss several issues related to the REB therapist's tasks in Chapter 6, including those related to the potency of therapeutic tasks and therapist skills.

The interactive nature of the four domains

While I have discussed the four domains of the working alliance separately in this chapter, they are not distinct in that each domain interacts with every other domain in practice. Similarly, while I will discuss each domain in a separate chapter as it relates to the effective practice of REBT, please bear in mind the dynamic and interactive nature of the four domains.

3 Bonds and the working alliance in REBT

In the previous chapter it was noted that the bonds domain of the working alliance points to the interpersonal connectedness between therapist and client. Such connectedness is enhanced when the REB therapist:

- encourages the client to feel safe, trust them and have faith in their expertise
- creates a sense of teamwork with the client
- demonstrates the 'core conditions' for client development
- adopts an appropriate interactive stance with the client
- varies their therapeutic style to accommodate the client's preferences
- varies the base of their influence to accommodate the client's preferences
- works with transference and counter-transference to help the client.

This chapter will now discuss these seven factors.

The REB therapist encourages the client to feel safe, trust them and have faith in their expertise

Therapy sessions will be of little value to clients if they do not feel safe in the therapeutic relationship, and if they do not trust their therapist or have faith in their expertise. Imagine how much therapeutic progress you would make if you were a client working with a therapist under such conditions?

Similarly, I consider that three fundamental tasks for REB therapists are to help their clients to feel safe and to communicate that they are competent and trustworthy. There are three important ways in which I believe they can do these tasks most effectively:

- The first involves the REB therapist clearly stating and explaining the main components of REBT theory and practice. This helps the client to know what the process entails and to thus feel safe in the therapeutic relationship – more so given that they also know they have a say in this relationship.
- The second involves the REB therapist giving full and serious consideration to the principle of informed consent. This means not only that the therapist explains REBT concepts and the nature of their therapeutic plans and strategies (i.e. the 'informed' component of informed consent), but also that the therapist actively seeks the client's consent to proceed (i.e. the 'consent' component of informed consent).
- The final way involves the therapist establishing what I call the 'reflection process'. This involves the therapist encouraging the client – at significant junctures – to step back and reflect on what has been happening between them. This helps the client to recognise that they have a say in the therapeutic relationship and that the option is always there for either of them to access the reflection process to discuss any matter. I will address this more fully later in the chapter.

The REB therapist creates a sense of teamwork with the client

REBT is founded on teamwork between the therapist (who contributes expertise relating to the REBT model of psychological disturbance) and the client (who contributes expertise relating to their own experience).

There are three ways that the therapist can help to create a team spirit in their work with the client:

- establishing an agenda with the client for each therapy session
- establishing what I call the 'reflection process' (Dryden, 1989) with the client
- establishing a problem list with the client.

Establishing a session agenda with the client

The creation of a session agenda is not usually considered to be a typical component of REBT sessions. However, I find that it can be helpful to develop a sense of teamwork and to use session time efficiently.

The use of session agendas can be traced back to Beck et al.'s (1979) pioneering work relating to the cognitive therapy of depression.

Where they are used by REB therapists, they involve the following considerations.

Providing a reason for the use of session agendas with the client

Here, the therapist explains that setting a session agenda at the beginning of the session:

- helps the client choose how to spend time in the session and ensures that they are devoting the most time to their most pressing issue
- ensures that the therapist and client are 'on the same' page during the session
- provides the therapist with an opportunity to cover important issues such as reviewing past homework tasks and negotiating new tasks to enable the client to get the most from therapy between sessions.

Having provided a rationale for the use of a session agenda, the therapist encourages the client to voice any reservations about using an agenda-based approach to sessions, takes seriously any concerns expressed and responds respectfully. The therapist might suggest using a session agenda to see how the client gets on with it but will drop its use if the client continues to find it unhelpful.

What a session agenda covers

A session agenda usually covers the following:

- the client's report on any assignment that the client has agreed to do in the preceding week
- the problem the client wants to focus on most during the session
- any additional issues the client wants to discuss
- the negotiation of an assignment based on what was covered in the session that the client agrees to do before the next session
- the client's feedback on the session that they have just had.

Creating and maintaining the reflection process with the client

REB therapists can encourage a sense of teamwork by suggesting to clients that they create and maintain a communication channel that I call the 'reflection process' (Dryden, 1989). This involves identifying something that they are experiencing or discussing that they would like to step back and reflect upon, from a more objective perspective. The items that the therapist and client usually refer to in the reflection process are ones either that they experience as problematic or that they feel would benefit from further objective discussion.

As also noted in the previous section about agenda-setting, it is important that the REB therapist justifies the establishment of the reflection process. When the therapist has provided a reason for the use of this type of communication, it is similarly helpful to encourage the client to mention any reservations they may have about using such a process and to respond to any such concerns. Clearly, it would be inappropriate for the REB therapist to continue using the reflection process if the client does not find it helpful or conducive to teamwork.

Establishing a problem list with the client

A third main way in which the REB therapist can promote teamwork is to encourage their client to generate a problem list. The client can use this to list the problems they wish to address in REBT, and can go on to add and remove problems from the list during the course of their therapy. The therapist's role involves working with the client on problems that the client has identified on their current list. This helps to ensure that they both keep focused on the client's priorities, and that the client is encouraged to work on such problems until they cease to be problems.

It is also worth mentioning here that REBT views clients' problems as closely connected to their goals for change. I will revisit the issue of dealing with problems in the chapter on 'goals' (see Chapter 5).

The REB therapist demonstrates the 'core conditions' for client development

When I discussed the bonds domain of the working alliance in Chapter 2, I outlined what has come to be known as the three 'core conditions' of empathy, genuineness and respect and the role they play in therapy. By way of recap, when the therapist demonstrates an empathic understanding of the client's problems, is genuine in the therapeutic encounter and shows unconditional positive regard for the client as a person, *and*, most importantly, when the client also experiences these 'core conditions', then the client will tend to move towards more healthy psychological functioning.

Rogers' (1957) original stance was that these 'core conditions' are necessary and sufficient for positive therapeutic change. This position similarly implies that these conditions need to be present and that client development can occur without any other conditions. In contrast, REBT approaches this from a more flexible perspective (Ellis, 1959) where the presence of such conditions is often considered to be desirable but neither necessary nor sufficient for clients to progress. The core conditions are not important for their own sake in REBT, but because they set the stage for subsequent technical and strategic work with the client.

This aligns with my personal view, which also reflects the working alliance position, in that these 'core conditions' are often important for most but not all clients. In this respect, the task of the REB therapist is to increase and decrease the emphasis on certain conditions with different clients to ascertain the most effective and personalised therapeutic bond with each client. Having made this point, I will now discuss each of the 'core conditions' and their role in REBT.

Demonstrating empathy from an REBT perspective: drawing on the ABC framework and an expanded view of empathy

For illustration purposes, I will consider the REBT approach to demonstrating empathy in the context of a client discussing a specific situation in which they have experienced their problem. Wessler and Wessler (1980) describe such a situation as 'an emotional episode'. A person-centred therapist would attempt to communicate to the client that they understood their experience during this emotional episode. An REB therapist would similarly endeavour to communicate this to the client, but would draw on REBT's *ABC* framework (see Chapter 1) while doing so. For example, an REB therapist would find the use of terms such as 'experience' overly vague. They would break this term down into its component parts (with reference to the *ABC* model) to convey to the client that they understand:

- how the client felt at *C*
- the inferences the client made at *A*
- the possible rigid and/or extreme basic attitudes the client might have been holding at *B* about *A*
- how the client acted or felt like acting at *C*
- how the client was thinking at *C* (these are known as the thinking consequences of holding the rigid and/or extreme attitudes at *B*).

In practice this may involve the therapist saying something to the client along the lines of:

'I get the impression that you felt hurt [emotional *C*] when you thought your friend had let you down [*A*]. You seem to have withdrawn into yourself when you felt hurt [behavioural *C*] and started thinking you wouldn't trust people again [thinking *C*]. I'm wondering whether your attitude towards being let down was along the lines of "this isn't something I would do to her, so she absolutely shouldn't have done this to me" [rigid attitude at *B*]?'

However, note that the REB therapist would be using the *ABC* framework implicitly and not explicitly with the client at this stage.

The way in which the REB therapist approaches this client's 'emotional episode' differs from the approach adopted by therapists from other therapeutic backgrounds in that the REB therapist is using the *ABC* framework to convey empathy. This involves the REB therapist drawing upon an external frame of reference to show the client that they understand their internal frame of reference. Furthermore, while other approaches to therapy emphasise affective empathy (i.e. conveying that the therapist understands how the client feels), REBT emphasises 'cognitive-affective-behavioural' empathy (i.e. conveying that the therapist understands how the client feels, thinks and acts and, where relevant, the attitudes that underpin this integrated response).

Demonstrating respect from an REBT perspective: unconditional acceptance

The second 'core condition' that I would like to consider here is therapist respect or – as it is more commonly referred to in the REBT literature – 'unconditional acceptance'. When an REB therapist shows their client that they accept them unconditionally, they are demonstrating that they view their client as a complex, in flux, fallible and unrateable human being and that they hold this attitude unconditionally – even when the client acts very badly.

Therefore, if the client informs the REB therapist that they have done something that is objectively bad, such as getting a colleague into trouble, the therapist endeavours to show the client that while what they did was certainly bad, they are complex and fallible. The therapist then suggests the need to understand this bad behaviour in the context of the client's frame of mind at the time. In this instance, the client had felt very angry towards their colleague and decided to get them into trouble as an act of revenge.

In such cases, the REB therapist is striving to a) demonstrate an attitude of unconditional acceptance in the way they treat the client and b) teach the client the principles of unconditional acceptance so that they may apply acceptance attitudes to themselves.

The distinction between the notion of unconditional positive regard/prizing/respect as used in person-centred therapy, and many other therapies, and unconditional acceptance as used in REBT is that the former advocates a positive global evaluation of the person, while the latter advocates a non-evaluative attitude that acknowledges that the nature of the person is complex, fallible and fluid while allowing for evaluation of aspects of the person. The disturbance-creating features of attitudes towards self/others/life are their conditionality (e.g. 'I am worthwhile if...').[1] Therefore, when REBT clients prefer to strive for unconditional positive self-regard rather than unconditional self-acceptance, this is fine given that the unconditionality of the attitude is to the fore.

The issue of therapist warmth in REBT

Unconditional positive regard or respect is sometimes referred to as 'non-possessive warmth'. Whereas Albert Ellis (the founder of REBT) retained his original position (1959) that the 'core conditions' in therapy may be desirable but not necessary for positive therapeutic change, he took a more critical view regarding therapist warmth in relation to REBT (Ellis & Dryden, 1985). For example, he considered that although clients seem to value this 'warmth' condition, it can serve to reinforce clients' dire needs for approval and encourage them to become more, as opposed to less, anxious about the possibility of losing approval in the future – not just their therapist's approval, but also the approval of other people in general (see Ellis & Dryden, 1985). This consideration was reflected in Ellis's work with his clients. For example, in a study by DiGiuseppe, Leaf and Linscott (1993), the authors reported that Ellis's clients perceived him to be less warm and intimate than did clients who saw other REB therapists. That is to say that Ellis minimised being warm with his clients in contrast to other REB therapists. This point also serves to counter a fairly common misconception of REBT – i.e. that all REB therapists develop relationships with their clients in the manner of Albert Ellis.

Genuineness and self-disclosure from an REBT perspective

The 'core condition' of genuineness is sometimes referred to as congruence and sometimes as openness. These terms share in common the following features:

---

1 REBT and person-centred therapy see 'conditions of worth' as lying at the core of much ego disturbance.

- The therapist does not hide behind a role or façade.
- The therapist is consistent between what they experience and what they disclose – both verbally and non-verbally.
- The therapist is willing to be honest about their experience with their clients.

With regard to therapist disclosure based on genuine experience, REB therapists are guided by two REBT principles. The first is that they will only disclose aspects of their experience that may be relevant to therapy if they consider that doing so will not be to the detriment of their client. The second is that not all clients will appreciate their therapist disclosing their personal experiences. Therefore, if an REB therapist is thinking about disclosing things but has not been invited to do so, it is important to first check with the client that they want to hear about their experiences before actually disclosing them. When the client has given such permission, the REB therapist will limit their self-disclosing to situations in which they:

- have previously experienced the problem with which the client is also struggling
- initially disturbed themself by having similar rigid and extreme attitudes to those held by the client
- then changed these attitudes and, importantly, where they can
- then show the client how they went on to change these attitudes, and how the client can similarly do so.

After self-disclosing, it is important that the therapist invites the client to provide them with feedback about, for example, ways in which they may, or may not, have found this helpful.

Genuineness and bond variation

A tenet of working alliance theory is that REB therapists should vary their bond with their clients, but that they should also do this in a genuine manner. The multimodal therapist Arnold Lazarus (1989) called the therapist who tailors the therapy relationship an 'authentic chameleon'. An important consideration here is that if it is indicated that the REB therapist vary their contribution to the bond in a way that takes them out of their comfort zone or beyond their repertoire, then it would be appropriate for the therapist to be true to themselves, rather than attempt to vary their approach in a non-genuine manner. The therapist may need to negotiate with the client in this respect, and to refer the client on if the therapist is unable in good faith to work with the client.

The REB therapist adopts an appropriate interactive stance with the client

In Chapter 2, I noted that REB therapists are initially inclined to assume an active-directive interactive stance. However, as REB therapy progresses, they gradually move towards what I call a 'prompting' interactive stance that encourages their clients to assume more responsibility for the therapeutic work. It is important – from a working alliance perspective – that the REB therapist explains their proposed stance to the client, and that they elicit the client's cooperation before proceeding. If a client has any reservations about the proposed stance, then it is important that the REB therapist addresses them.

Active-directive interactive stance

After initially inviting the client to tell them why they are seeking therapy and what they hope to achieve from it, the REB therapist usually adopts an active-directive interactive stance. However, the therapist will first discuss with the client the rationale for adopting such a stance and its implications for the client's participation in the therapeutic process. As indicated throughout, the therapist elicits and deals with any doubts, reservations and objections the client may have – in this case regarding the therapist adopting an active-directive interactive stance.

There are several reasons why REB therapists tend to adopt an active-directive interactive stance with their clients, particularly in the early stage/s of therapy:

• The REB therapist uses a specific *ABC* framework to assess the client's problems. In order to do so they have to actively direct the client to provide the relevant information that will help the therapist make an accurate assessment of the client's problems (see Chapter 1).
• The REB therapist promotes the examination of rigid and extreme attitudes. In doing so, they actively direct the client to consider several issues before encouraging the client to strive to strengthen their alternative flexible and non-extreme attitudes.
• The REB therapist encourages the setting of homework assignments. To help the client to get the most out of homework assignments, the therapist actively directs the client to salient information concerning negotiating and reviewing such assignments.

- The REB therapist helps the client to deal with obstacles to change. In order to do so, they actively direct the client to identify the source of obstacles and to deal with it.

Working alliance considerations

Working alliance theory contends that not all clients will respond positively to an active-directive therapeutic stance. In this respect, the REB therapist can adjust their stance to effectively help a wide range of clients and, indeed, is particularly careful to monitor the impact of their active-directive stance on clients. Therefore, when working with clients who are, for example, highly sensitive to what they experience as threats to their sense of autonomy, the REB therapist would take care to emphasise client choice in their interactions. On the other hand, when working with clients who are more passive and dependent, the REB therapist would assume a stance that particularly encourages client direction and activity. Therefore, while it may be difficult to imagine practising REBT with a non-directive stance, REB therapists can, and do, vary the extent of their activity and directiveness according to different clients. As noted previously, they also vary the extent of their activity and directiveness according to the phase of the counselling process. That is, the REB therapist will usually be less active and directive during the latter stages of the process as clients assume greater personal responsibility for implementing REBT strategies and work towards becoming their own therapists. I will elaborate on this issue below.

Prompting interactive stance

The REB therapist usually starts to adopt a prompting interactive stance with the client when the client has developed skills in using REBT independently. At such a stage, if the client mentions a new emotional episode related to their nominated problem or another problem, the therapist prompts the client to draw on what they have already learned about REBT, rather than adopting the more active-directive stance associated with an earlier stage of therapy when clients are new to REBT. Similarly, just as the active-directive stance is appropriate for a client who at the outset knows little about this approach and has to be directed to use and then learn it, the prompting stance is appropriate for a more REBT-experienced client. The timely application of the appropriate stance with the client is a hallmark of the REB therapist who is mindful of the working alliance in the way they adopt one or other stance.

As with the active-directive interactive stance, it is important that the REB therapist provides the client with a rationale for using a prompting stance. In the latter case, the REB therapist would discuss the client's readiness to take the lead in using REBT during the session, with the therapist providing any necessary prompts. Prior to obtaining the client's consent to this shift in approach, the therapist elicits and responds to any doubts, reservations and objections that the client may have about taking the lead with the support of any necessary prompts from the therapist.

The REB therapist varies their therapeutic style to accommodate the client's preferences

Based on my experience, the majority of REB therapists are inclined to adopt a relatively informal therapeutic style with their clients. On the other hand, REBT theory and practice does not discourage therapists from adopting a more formal therapeutic style, and working alliance theory indicates that REB therapists adapt their degree of formality according to their clients' particular preferences.

A pertinent example here concerns the way in which humour is used in REBT. Albert Ellis tended to use humour in his REBT practice, just as I do, although I also know quite a few REB therapists who do not use it. The use of humour is based on considerations of both therapist genuineness and client preferences. Therefore, I believe that therapists should avoid using humour if they cannot use it in a genuine manner and if their clients do not appreciate therapists using it in therapy. Therapists' use of humour can otherwise greatly facilitate the practice and process of REBT.

The REB therapist varies the base of their influence to accommodate the client's preferences

I mentioned in Chapter 2 that therapy can be viewed as a process of influence. In this respect, the REB therapist exerts their influence in an ethical context supported by the above-noted safeguards: clarity of communication about REBT theory and the therapy process; operationalising the principle of informed consent, and use of the reflection process. From an influence perspective, the explicit aim of the REB therapist is to encourage the client to develop flexible and non-extreme attitudes rather than rigid and extreme attitudes towards life's adversities.

The way in which Albert Ellis (the founder of REBT) practised therapy was from an influence base that emphasised *expertise*. This is often a particularly effective influence base, given that many people are more ready to be influenced by others when they value their expertise. Similarly, many clients may attach far more importance to their therapist having expertise they value than, for example, to whether they *like* their therapist. However, there are other clients who are more likely to be influenced by people whom they *like*, and who attach less importance to their therapist's expert status.

As is the case with other areas of the bonds domain, working alliance theory suggests that REB therapists consider their clients' particular influence preferences, and adapt the base of their attempts to influence them accordingly.

The REB therapist works with transference and counter-transference to help the client

I will conclude this chapter about bonds between REB therapists and their clients by considering the concepts of transference and countertransference. While these concepts stem from psychoanalytic therapeutic approaches (see Jacobs, 2017), they also signpost phenomena that require fuller consideration from a working alliance perspective in REBT. For example, building on Chapter 2, these terms recognise that both the client and therapist bring to their therapeutic relationship tendencies to perceive, feel and act towards other people in ways that are influenced by their previous interactions with significant others.

Working with transference in REBT

There is a social-cognitive model of transference put forward by Miranda and Andersen (2007) which is relevant to the REB therapist's management of this phenomenon. The model suggests they might approach this as follows:

- First, ask the client to name and describe significant others with specific reference to aspects of their interpersonal relating.
- Having identified the client's mental representations of interpersonal relating, the therapist can recognise when these are activated in the therapeutic relationship and then help the client to perceive the link between their present response to the therapist and their representations of significant others. In so doing, it is important to identify – with the client's assistance – specific activation cues in the therapist's behaviour.

- I also suggest that the therapist apologises for any unintentional sensitivity. This helps the client to use the reflection process which is so important when transferential experiences are being processed.

Working with counter-transference in REBT

In Chapter 2, I mentioned that counter-transference reactions can be helpful as well as unhelpful. Both Ellis (2002) and Leahy (2007) identify rigid and extreme attitudes which make REB therapists susceptible to experiencing *unhelpful* counter-transference responses. Such attitudes include need for approval, intolerance and emotional inhibition. In order to acknowledge anti-therapeutic reactions to clients that stem from such attitudes, it is important that the therapist also has attitudes of unconditional self-acceptance, self-compassion and humility. Therapists are also particularly vulnerable to feeling ashamed about experiencing unhelpful reactions (which may lead them to deny their existence to others and themselves) – more so if they hold rigid and extreme attitudes about what it means to be a therapist (e.g. 'Because I am an REB therapist, I absolutely should not have negative reactions to my clients'). It is important for REB therapists to deal with rigid and extreme attitudes in a similar way to how they would approach them with their clients. The matter of dealing with counter-transference does also lead to consideration of the role of personal therapy for REBT practitioners and the appropriate nature of such personal therapy.

With respect to *helpful* counter-transference reactions in REBT, these happen when the therapist experiences a tendency to think, feel and act in a similar way to others in the client's life. After acknowledging this tendency, the therapist can go on to utilise it, in conjunction with the reflection process, to first help the client to understand the impact of their behaviour on others and to then identify and address the rigid and extreme attitudes underpinning such behaviour. An example would be when a therapist is working with a client who complains that others, including the therapist, don't listen to them, whereas the therapist had previously experienced frustration because the client did not listen to them. By referring the concern to the reflection process and disclosing their reactions, the therapist helps the client to recognise the association between the client not listening to others and others not listening to them. The therapist then goes on to help the client to identify and address the rigid and extreme attitudes underpinning their own non-listening behaviour.

In the next chapter, I will consider REBT in the 'views' domain of the working alliance.

4 Views and the working alliance in REBT

In this chapter, I will cover the following topics:

* introducing the REBT view on psychological problems to clients
* introducing the REBT view on therapy and therapeutic tasks to clients
* introducing the REBT view on therapeutic change to clients
* when to seek informed consent from clients in REBT.

Introduction

In his formative article on the working alliance, Bordin (1979) put forward a tripartite model of the alliance in which the three components were bonds, goals and tasks. It later occurred to me that this model was missing a component that captures the therapist's and client's views on key aspects of the therapeutic process. Therefore I added a component called 'views' (Dryden, 2006; 2011).

From a views perspective, the REB therapist and the client need to agree on the following:

* *How the client's problems are understood.* This involves the therapist eliciting the client's view of their own problem and outlining REBT's view of psychological disturbance and its associated *ABC* framework. The main reason for doing this is that it helps to make sense of the client's problems and the factors that maintain them. Similarly, working alliance theory emphasises the importance of the therapist incorporating the client's view into the REBT view whenever they can.
* *What will be helpful to the client.* In order to establish this, the client needs to indicate what they think will help them, and the therapist needs to describe the therapeutic nature of REBT and the ways

in which the client might find it helpful. Again, working alliance theory contends that the therapist and client need to have sufficient agreement in this area for REBT to have a chance of success.

- *The tasks that both have to perform during REBT.* The emphasis here is on the REB therapist being clear with the client about the nature of their respective tasks during their work together. The way in which the therapist communicates this will depend on the particular client and what the client is ready to understand.
- *REBT's view of the change process.* It is essential that the client understands what the change process is likely to entail from an REBT perspective.

Introducing the REBT view on psychological problems to clients

It is very important that the therapist has an open discussion with their client regarding their respective views on psychological problems. There are two main reasons that the therapist and client need to have an explicit discussion about this:

- *Ethical considerations.* The purpose of the discussion here is to enable the client to give or withhold their informed consent to proceed with therapy. Informed consent is a founding ethical principle in most, or even all, of the codes of ethics and conduct for counselling and psychotherapy professionals. Furthermore, there is a view – which emerged from social work in the United States – that a client *only* becomes a client when they have given their informed consent to proceed with a form of help that has been outlined to them and that they actively want to utilise. Until that point, it is best to consider them to be an applicant for help (Seabury, Seabury & Garvin, 2011). Similarly, REBT espouses the informed consent principle, and maintains that a potential client cannot be expected to give informed consent if they have not been appropriately informed. Therefore, from an REBT perspective, a person only becomes a client if a) they understand the REBT view of psychological problems, particularly as this view relates to their concerns, and b) they understand the REBT approach to assisting with these concerns, and c) they want to make use of these views and approaches in their therapy and give their informed consent to proceed.
- *Practical considerations.* There are also pragmatic reasons for the REB therapist outlining to the client the REBT view of psychological problems and engaging them in a discussion about their respective views. As noted by Barker and his colleagues (Barker

et al., 1990; Pistrang & Barker, 1992), the closer the therapist's and client's views on psychological problems, the more robust the working alliance in this domain and in general. While it might be expected that the therapist and client will have different views, this is not necessarily problematic unless their views are radically different. In the latter case, REBT may not be a viable treatment for that client and, if so, the therapist would better serve the client's interests by arranging a referral to a practitioner whose approach is more closely aligned with the client's view.

If we are agreed about the importance of the REB therapist introducing the REBT view on psychological problems, then some questions that this raises include the following:

- When should the therapist do this?
- Should the therapist use the client's problem in their explanation or not?
- How should the therapist explain the REBT model of psychological problems?
- How should the therapist deal with clients who hold different views of psychological problems?

I will discuss these issues in turn.

When should the therapist introduce the REBT view of psychological problems?

Woods (1991) developed a unique approach to explaining the REBT model. This involved him providing the client with a detailed outline of the model, with reference to charts to illustrate his points, *before* the client had had an opportunity to tell him about the nature of their problems.

It is now unlikely that REB therapists would adopt such a radical approach. This is because most would hold the view that a person who seeks help expects to tell their therapist about their problem in their first session. Therefore, it is more appropriate for the therapist to explain the REBT model *after* the client has had an opportunity to discuss their problems and how they understand them. In addition, the therapist needs to know what the client's problem is if they are going to incorporate this as content when they outline the REBT model.

Clearly, if the client were to become very distressed while describing their problem(s), then it would be appropriate for the therapist to delay introducing the REBT model. Indeed, there is an element of judgement involved when it comes to determining an appropriate time to explain the model. It is also not a decision that the therapist needs to make alone, as this issue can be put on the session agenda, and the therapist and client can also talk about when to discuss the model in a particular session – which is also a good teamwork-building strategy (see Chapter 3).

Having considered the matter of introducing REBT in the first session, it should be noted that some REB therapists additionally send introductory material to prospective clients, or to clients who have booked a first appointment (i.e. ahead of the first session). I include in Box 4.1 an example of what such material outlines about the REBT view of psychological problems and the way in which it addresses these problems.

Box 4.1 What is Rational Emotive Behaviour Therapy?

There are a number of approaches to therapy and it is important that you understand something of the one that I practise which is known as Rational Emotive Behaviour Therapy (REBT). REBT is based on an old idea attributed to Epictetus, a Roman philosopher, who said that: 'Men are disturbed not by things, but by their views of things.' In REBT, we have modified this and say that: 'People are disturbed not by things, but by their rigid and extreme attitudes towards things.' Once they have disturbed themselves, they then try to get rid of their disturbed feelings in ways that ultimately serve to maintain their problems.

As an REB therapist I will help you to identify, examine and change the rigid and extreme attitudes that we argue underpin your emotional problems and to develop alternative flexible and non-extreme attitudes. I will also help you to examine the ways in which you have tried to help yourself that haven't worked and encourage you to develop and practise more effective, longer-lasting strategies. At the beginning of therapy, we will consider your problems one at a time and I will teach you a framework which will help you to break down your problems into their constituent parts. I will also teach you a variety of methods for examining and changing your rigid and extreme attitudes and a variety of methods to help you to consolidate and strengthen your alternative flexible and non-extreme attitudes. As therapy proceeds, I will help you to take increasing responsibility for using these methods, and my ultimate aim is to help you to become your own therapist. As this happens, we will meet less frequently until you feel you can cope on your own.

Explaining the REBT model: Should the therapist use the client's material or not?

When considering how to present the REBT model, a choice needs to be made about whether to relate this to the client's stated problem or not. An advantage of incorporating the client's problem as content can be that it helps the client to see how the REBT view is applicable to understanding their particular problem. However, this approach can also have two disadvantages. The first is that, after disclosing their problem, the client may not be in a sufficiently objective frame of mind to derive much benefit from a description of how the model applies to their problem. The second disadvantage is that, if the client's view of their problem differs from the REBT view, the client may be more inclined to resist the REBT view when it is related to their problem than when it is presented more generally (i.e. without reference to their problem). As above, this is not a decision that the therapist needs to make alone; it is one that needs to be discussed with the client.

How should the therapist explain the REBT model of psychological problems?

The literature contains several examples of how to explain the REBT model to clients. For example, Ellis often used the 'Money Model' in his first session with clients, and I show how I use this model in Box 4.2.

Box 4.2 Explaining the REBT model of psychological problems: the Money Model

Windy: Imagine that you hold an attitude where you prefer to have a minimum of £11 in your pocket at all times, but it's not necessary that you have this amount. While holding this attitude, you discover you only have £10, how will you feel?
Client: Concerned.
Windy: Right. Or you'd feel disappointed, but you wouldn't kill yourself. Right?
Client: Right.
Windy: OK. Now this time imagine that you hold the attitude that you absolutely <u>have to</u> have a minimum £11 in your pocket at all times. You <u>must</u> have it, it is a <u>necessity</u>. You <u>must</u>, you <u>must</u>, you <u>must</u> have a minimum of £11, and again you look and you find you only have £10. How will you feel?

Client: Very anxious.

Windy: Right, or depressed. Now remember it's the same £10, but a different attitude. OK, now this time you still have the same attitude. You have to have a minimum of £11 at all times, you must. It's absolutely essential. But this time you look in your pocket and find that you've got £12. How will you feel?

Client: Relieved, content.

Windy: Right. But with that same attitude that you have to have a minimum of £11 at all times – something occurs to you that leads you to becoming very anxious again. What do you think that would be?

Client: What if I lose £2?

Windy: Right. What if I lose £2, what if I spend £2, what if I get robbed? That's right. Now the moral of this model – which applies to just about all humans, rich or poor, black or white, male or female, young or old, in the past or in the future, assuming humans are still human – is that people make themselves miserable if they don't get what they think they must get, but they are also panicked when they do get what they think they must get – because of the must. For even if they have what they think they must have, they could always lose it.

Client: So I have no chance to be happy when I don't have what I think I must have – and little chance of remaining unanxious when I do have it?

Windy: Right! Your musturbation will get you nowhere – except depressed or panicked!

How should the therapist deal with clients' views of psychological problems when these differ from the REBT view?

There can be occasions when a client expresses a view about psychological problems that diverges from the REBT perspective. The REB therapist will demonstrate respect for the client's alternative view and will offer justification for the *ABC* view in the spirit of inviting further discussion. In situations when the difference between the client's and REB therapist's views concerns the determinants of the client's problem, the therapist respects the client's view and encourages the client to compare their different views. The most frequent difference regarding problem determinants is when the client believes that *A* causes *C*, and I will illustrate how the REB therapist approaches this below.

Dealing with the client's *A–C* **view.** When a client puts forward an *A* causes *C* view of psychological problems, they are assuming that the adversity that they faced at *A* (with *A* being either the event itself or the client's inference about that event) caused their dysfunctional responses at *C*. This contrasts with the REBT view which maintains that it is the client's rigid and extreme basic attitudes at *B* towards the adversity at *A* that primarily determine their dysfunctional responses at *C*.

One way in which the REB therapist can approach these contrasting views is first to summarise the client's *A–C* view to the client's satisfaction, then put forward the REBT model (which crucially adds basic attitudes at *B*) and then encourage the client to reflect upon which approach provides the most effective explanation of their emotional problem at *C*. If the client is undecided, the therapist can additionally show the client that when they change their basic attitudes towards the same *A*, they will then usually experience a different emotion at *C*. This helps to highlight, for the client, the significance of basic attitudes at *B*. However, it is also important to emphasise to the client that they are correct in their view that *A* *contributes* to their emotional problem at *C*. Once a client understands that a contribution is different from a cause (or primary determinant), they are usually reassured that their views can be incorporated into the REBT viewpoint and that their views have been given serious consideration.

Introducing the REBT view on the therapy process and therapeutic tasks to clients

After the therapist has helped the client to understand how rigid and extreme attitudes contribute to their problems, it is reasonably straight-forward to help them to recognise that the main focus in REBT is to encourage the client to stand back and examine such attitudes as well as the alternative set of flexible and non-extreme attitudes and to deter-mine which set of attitudes will help them to deal with their problems more effectively.

It can be useful for the therapist to make use of a client's therapy preferences when explaining REBT's view of therapy and therapeutic tasks. For example, if the client has previously been in therapy, the therapist can ask them what they experienced as being helpful and unhelpful about that therapy. The therapist can then incorporate the helpful aspects into their explanation of the REBT view of therapy and also illustrate how REBT does not incorporate aspects that the client previously found to be unhelpful. When relating their explanation to what the client is, and is not, hoping for, it is obviously important that the therapist avoids presenting a false picture of REBT. If the client wants something that REBT cannot provide, then it is vital that the therapist is clear that this is something REBT cannot offer.

When explaining the REBT view of therapy, I recommend that the therapist stresses the points below:

- The therapist needs to help the client to clearly identify their problems, and the client needs to be as transparent as possible about their problems. The therapist helps the client to deal with their problems one at a time.
- The client needs (as discussed above) to understand and apply REBT's model of psychological disturbance to their problems. Specifically, the client needs to recognise that their difficulties mainly stem from the rigid and extreme attitudes they hold towards the adversities that feature in their problems. The client also needs to mention any doubts, reservations and objections they might have about this model, and the therapist needs to address these in a respectful and straightforward manner.
- The therapist initially needs to help the client to set goals with respect to these adversities, and then to recognise that in order to achieve these goals they need to hold an alternative set of flexible and non-extreme attitudes towards such adversities.
- The therapist needs to help the client to stand back and examine both sets of attitudes and to make a commitment to developing the flexible and non-extreme set of attitudes.
- The therapist needs to help the client to generate and implement an action plan that draws on a range of cognitive, imaginal, behavioural and emotive techniques to strengthen their conviction in their flexible and non-extreme attitudes. The client needs to carry out any associated between-session work on a regular basis, and this will involve the client tolerating the discomfort of facing the adversities that feature in their problems.
- The client needs to learn to apply REBT self-change skills and to take increasing responsibility for their progress as therapy unfolds, until they can deal with their problems on their own.

As illustrated in the points above, in addition to outlining the REBT view of therapy, the therapist needs to outline to the client the tasks that they each have to perform during the course of REBT. All such material needs to be discussed with the client, and the therapist also needs to respond in a respectful and genuine manner to any questions or concerns that the client might have (see also Chapter 6).

Introducing the REBT view on therapeutic change to clients

If the client has an unrealistic view of therapeutic change, then this will have a negative impact on their participation in the change process. Therefore, it is important that the REB therapist provides a clear outline of the REBT view of therapeutic change, and that this outline distinguishes between realistic and unrealistic views concerning the change journey. For example, many clients hold the limiting and unrealistic view that intellectual insight into their rigid and extreme attitudes is sufficient for meaningful change to occur. I will expand upon why this view is unrealistic below.

Two types of insight

In a seminal article, Ellis (1963) made an important distinction between two types of insight in REBT: 'intellectual insight' and 'emotional insight'. This article suggested that:

*   When a client has 'intellectual insight', they have an intellectually based understanding that their rigid and extreme attitudes are false, illogical and largely unconstructive and that their flexible and non-extreme attitudes are true, logical and largely constructive. However, this insight has little impact on the client's feelings and behaviour.
*   When a client has 'emotional insight', the client has an emotionally based strong conviction that their rigid and extreme attitudes are again false, illogical and largely unconstructive and that their flexible and non-extreme attitudes are again true, logical and largely constructive. In contrast to 'intellectual insight', 'emotional insight' has an impact on the client's feelings and behaviour.

Based on the above, intellectual insight has little impact on the client's feelings and behaviour and therefore, while initially important, it is unlikely to be of much further help to the client with respect to pursuing their healthy goals. Similarly, it is important that the REB therapist distinguishes between intellectual and emotional insight when they explain the REBT change process to the client.

When to introduce the REBT view of therapeutic change to the client

There are two main occasions when the REB therapist can outline the REBT view of therapeutic change to their client. The first is at the start of therapy and before the therapist seeks informed consent from the client. The second is when the client has given informed consent to proceed and after the client has achieved intellectual insight into their first presenting problem in therapy.

My own practice is to do this when the client has achieved such insight, but I will also do this with clients who prefer to understand the entire process of REBT before giving informed consent to proceed. As with other matters, the REB therapist does not make such a decision unilaterally but will share their thinking with the client and seek their view on the matter. Establishing a joint decision will strengthen the working alliance.

When to seek informed consent from clients in REBT

As indicated in this chapter, there are three main reasons why it is important for the REB therapist to explain the REBT view on various aspects of REBT theory and therapy. These are:

a) to strengthen the working alliance between therapist and client
b) to help the client understand key ideas and therefore get the most out of REBT
c) to enable the client to give informed consent to proceed.

This third reason raises the further question of how much information the therapist should provide before the client can be said to be in a position to give their informed consent to proceed. In this respect, I noted above that some clients, albeit a minority, will prefer to give such consent after they have understood all the aspects I have covered in this chapter. Such clients are usually inclined to be careful and hesitant to commit to things until they know all the relevant facts. It is important that REB therapists respect and do not pathologise such clients' preferences, and that they provide them with ample information and, if necessary, give them extended time to reflect on the matter of informed consent.

My view is that the minimum amount of information that a client needs to be given in order to be said to have given informed consent to proceed is the REBT views of psychological problems, and of therapy and therapeutic tasks.

In the next chapter, I will consider REBT skills in the goals domain of the working alliance.

5   Goals and the working alliance in REBT

In this chapter, I will consider the issue of goals in REBT with reference to the following considerations:

*   when to ask clients for their therapeutic goals in REBT
*   helping the client to develop a list of problems and goals informed by REBT theory
*   the changing nature of goals in the working alliance.

Introduction

As with other social activities, psychotherapy serves a *purpose*. Its main purpose is to help one of the participants (the client) to achieve something. While the other participant (the therapist) may also benefit from the meeting/s (e.g. benefit financially, or in terms of experiencing personal satisfaction from helping the client), I emphasise that the primary purpose of the psychotherapy encounter is for the client to achieve something from their sessions with their therapist.

Regarding *what* the client wants to achieve in therapy, it may seem – at least superficially – that the client is seeking relief from the psychological pain that led them to seek therapy. However, the issue of client goals is less straightforward when considered in the light of the REBT framework. I will attempt to address some of the complexity that surrounds the issue of goals within this chapter, and with reference to the working alliance in REBT.

When to ask the client for their goals

There are two main occasions when the REB therapist should ask the client to express their goals in therapy:

*   at the start of therapy (when goals may be discussed more generally)

- after the start of therapy, when they are assessing the client's problem (when goals can be discussed more specifically).

Asking for the client's goals at the start of therapy

When the REB therapist asks new clients what they want to achieve from therapy, clients will offer a range of responses that are usually problematic from an REBT perspective. In this section, I will outline the problematic nature of such responses and how the therapist can address them. In so doing, I will indicate which responses need to, and do not need to, be questioned when they arise.

The client's expressed goal is vague

The client may set a vague goal, such as 'I want to be happy', 'I want to get on with my life' or 'I want to get over my anxiety'. It is important that the REB therapist helps the client to make such goals more specific. A commonly used acronym in REBT and CBT represents an antidote to vague goals. It is SMART. Smart goals are those that are: specific, measurable, attainable, realistic and timely. The REB therapist keeps this acronym in mind when helping their client to set goals, albeit the goals may be expressed less specifically at the beginning of therapy than when the therapist has gone on to assess the client's problem with reference to the REBT framework.

The client wants to feel a disturbed emotion with less intensity

In this instance, the client may express their emotional goal along the lines of 'I want to feel less anxious'. Given that REBT considers anxiety to be an unhealthy negative emotion, it would help the client to remain disturbed, albeit with less intensity, if the therapist were to go along with this goal. At a minimum, what is needed here (unless the therapist considers this to be an appropriate time to proceed with a problem assessment) is for the client to be given help in setting a goal that involves them experiencing a healthy negative emotional response to the adversity at *A* rather than a diluted unhealthy negative emotional response to the same adversity.

The client wants to feel good or neutral about an adversity

Some clients state that their goal in therapy is to achieve a positive or neutral emotional state. However, when it is also recognised that the client's problematic emotional response is associated with a negative situation/

adversity, it is not realistic or appropriate to expect a client to feel good or neutral about that adversity. The REB therapist can discuss this perspective on the adversity with the client, while also helping them to see that they can choose between unhealthy negative and healthy negative emotional responses to that adversity. This is something that can be discussed with the client at the beginning of therapy or following the assessment of the client's problem. However, the important thing is that *when* it is discussed, the therapist helps the client to see that having healthy negative feelings about an adversity can help them to deal with the adversity if it *can* be changed or to adjust constructively to it if it *cannot* be changed.

The client expresses a personal development goal when they are disturbed

In the mid-1960s, Mahrer (1967) asked eminent psychotherapists to write chapters on what they considered to be the goals of psychotherapy. Mahrer found that the authors were essentially discussing two discrete sets of goals: overcoming disturbance (OD) goals and personal development (PD) goals. This important distinction is also applicable to REBT, which further argues that it is important to help the client to achieve their OD goals before they pursue their PD goals. Therefore, if a client states that they want to work towards a PD goal when it is clear that they are struggling with a problem about which they are disturbed, the REB therapist needs to help them to redirect their attention to *first* achieving their OD goal before they set out to achieve their PD goal. Asking a client whether it is better for them to achieve their PD goal when they are disturbed or when they are free from such disturbance usually helps them to see that the latter is the case. The therapist can address this issue with the client at the outset or when they come to assess their problem.

The client's goal is based on disturbance

An example of a disturbance-based goal is an anorexic client stating that their goal for therapy is to lose more weight. In cases such as this, the priority is to deal with the level of disturbance before setting concrete goals. This is an issue that needs to be addressed at the outset in order to avoid the therapist giving the client the impression that they will accept a goal that is based on disturbance.

The client wants to achieve a goal that is outside their control

Some clients may express goals in terms such as 'I want my father to change' or 'My goal is for the local council to find me a better flat'. These goals are for somebody or something to change that is outside of the client's control. For this reason, the REB therapist is advised not to accept these goals, but to renegotiate them so that their achievement falls within the client's power (for example, in terms of what the client is going to do differently to encourage their father to change or what the client is going to do to persuade the council to find them a better flat).

The REB therapist needs to renegotiate such goals at the outset. Otherwise, the client may get the false impression that the therapist will help them to directly change something they do not have it in their power to change. When the therapist is discussing this with the client, they need to be clear, for example, that while they cannot help the client to *change* another person, they can help the client to *influence* another person, as that is within the client's control. However, the therapist should also advise the client that the other person might resist their attempts to influence them, and might not change. If this seems likely, the therapist should offer the client an opportunity to set a goal based on the unchanging nature of *A*.

The client expresses a goal that someone else wants them to achieve

When the therapist asks the client what they want to achieve from REBT, they sometimes say something along the lines of 'My wife wants me to control my anger' or 'My boss wants me to be more confident'. In such instances, the therapist needs to ask the client what they think about the other person's opinion. Sometimes they may agree with the other person, in which case the client's goal is the same as the goal that the other person has for them. At other times, the client may disagree with the other person's goal for them, and the REB therapist will therefore need to discuss with the client what they do want to achieve. If the client is adamant that they do not have a problem, then it is not sensible to set a goal with them, or to proceed with therapy.

However, clients in such situations are often not sure about whether they have a problem or not. When this is the case, it is best for the REB therapist to help the client to accept and explore their ambivalence. If this exploration leads them to decide that they do, on balance, have a problem, then they can proceed with goal-setting.

Asking for the client's goals during problem assessment

In the section above, I focused on discussing the client's goal/s when they commence therapy. The other main point at which the REB therapist usually asks the client to set goals is when they are assessing the client's problem. The advantage of setting goals during problem assessment is that the client will see more clearly at this stage that they need their goals to be specifically set in response to the adversity at *A*. In short, their goals, if met, will help them to deal effectively with that adversity. Such considerations will be discussed in more detail below.

Helping the client to develop a list of problems and goals informed by REBT theory

My first point, in relation to the benefit of goal-setting during REBT problem assessment, demonstrates how the REB therapist helps the client to develop a list of problems and goals that are informed by REBT theory (Dryden, 2001; 2022).

Defining and formulating the client's problems with reference to the REBT framework[1]

In order to help the client to frame their problems from the REBT perspective, the REB therapist elicits the following from the client:

*   the context in which the problem typically occurs, if relevant
*   the main inferential theme at *A* about which the client disturbs themselves
*   the client's primary unhealthy negative emotion (UNE) at *C*
*   the client's dysfunctional behaviour or action tendency at *C*
*   the client's grossly distorted subsequent thinking at *C*, if relevant (see Chapter 1).

For example: 'Whenever people are late for a meeting with me [context], I get unhealthily angry [UNE at *C*] about their lack of respect for me [*A*]. I only wait for them for a minute [behavioural *C*] and think about how I can get my revenge on them [thinking *C*].'

Formulating and setting the client's goals with respect to their problems, with reference to the REBT framework[2]

Having helped the client to frame their problem/s from an REBT perspective, the REB therapist helps the client to set a goal with respect to

---

1 When working with a specific example of the client's problem, both the context and the *A* will be specific rather than general.
2 When setting goals with respect to a specific example of the client's problem, both the context and the *A* will be specific rather than general.

their problem and to put this into the REBT framework. In doing so, the REB therapist elicits the following information:

- the context in which the problem typically occurs, if relevant
- the main inferential theme at *A* about which the client disturbs themself
- the client's alternative healthy negative emotion (HNE) at *C*
- the client's alternative functional behaviour or action tendency at *C*
- the client's realistic subsequent thinking at *C*, if relevant (see Chapter 1).

For example: 'Whenever people are late for a meeting with me [context], I want to feel healthily angry rather than unhealthily angry [HNE is the desired new *C*] about their lack of respect for me [*A*]. I will wait for them for twenty minutes rather than leave after a minute [new behavioural *C*] and rather than think about how I can get my revenge on them, I will think about how to assert myself with them when they turn up [new thinking *C*].'

As can be seen from this and the previous section, the problem context and the inferential theme at *A* are the same when the therapist is working with the client to define their problem and, subsequently, to define their goals. However, when the therapist is setting goals with the client, healthy goal-related *Cs* are explicitly contrasted with unhealthy problem *Cs*. These two points are clearly shown in Table 5.1 and are also discussed in the two sections below.

The context and the A are the same in the client's problem and goal

There is a sound justification for the context and inferences being the same with respect to the client's problem and also their goal. This is based on REBT's contention that the best time either to modify the context in which the problem occurs, or to question the inference that the client has made at *A*, is when the client is in a healthy frame of mind. In order for the client to be in a healthy frame of mind, they have to hold flexible and non-extreme, as opposed to rigid and extreme, attitudes towards the adversity. Bearing in mind that the therapist and client usually frame problems and goals from an REBT perspective quite some time before the client has learned to identify, examine and change their rigid and extreme attitudes in favour of their alternative flexible and non-extreme attitudes, it is more realistic, when setting goals, to temporarily assume that the adversity (i.e. the context and the *A*) is real. It is

Table 5.1 **Example of goal-setting in REBT**

Context
People being late for a meeting with me

Inference at A
They are showing me lack of respect

Problem at C	Goals at C
Emotional C: Unhealthy anger Behavioural C: Only wait for a minute Cognitive C: Think about taking revenge	Emotional C: *Healthy anger* Behavioural C: *Wait for 20 mins* Cognitive C: *Think about asserting myself*

Note that the context and the inference at *A* are the same in the problem and the goals.

important that the REB therapist takes time to explain and discuss this rationale with the client.

Healthy goal-related Cs *are explicitly contrasted with unhealthy problem* Cs

If you compare the formulated problem with its formulated goal in the examples above, you can see that in the latter the healthy *C* (emotional, behavioural and thinking) is contrasted with the original unhealthy *C* (emotional, behavioural and thinking), and with reference to the phrase 'rather than'. In my view, it is important that the goal statement draws on such phrases as this helps the client to keep these contrasts in the forefront of their mind. This relates to a point I will consider in the next chapter, which is that attitude change in REBT is facilitated by two related, but contrasting, conditions. The first is when the client thinks and acts in ways that are consistent with their developing flexible and non-extreme attitudes. The second is when the client refrains from thinking and acting in ways that are consistent with their rigid and extreme attitudes. When these contrasts are included in the client's goal statement, it helps the client to convert their goal-related thinking and behavioural *C*s into actual thinking and behaviour.

Goals and the working alliance: a final word

Working alliance theory proposes that the alliance becomes stronger and the therapy becomes more effective under the following two conditions:

* when the therapist and client agree on the client's goals and these goals are in the client's best long-term interests
* when the client actively works towards these goals.

In this respect, it is important to bear in mind that client's goals are subject to change over the course of therapy. This is partly due to intervening life events and partly due to the therapist's and client's work together. Given such changes, it is important that the therapist does not assume that once a client has expressed their goals (generally at the beginning of therapy), these goals will apply throughout the process of therapy. Similarly, the therapist needs to keep themselves up to date on the state of the client's goals.

In the next and concluding chapter, I will consider the tasks domain of the REBT working alliance.

6 Tasks and the working alliance in REBT

Introduction

In Chapter 2 I noted that REBT is often portrayed as a technical approach to psychotherapy. I have hopefully shown in later chapters that REBT practitioners do more than merely implement therapeutic techniques. For example, in Chapter 3 I considered how the REB therapist attends to, nurtures and develops the bond between them and their client. In Chapter 4 I focused on the REB therapist's work in helping their client to understand and discuss their respective views about salient aspects of REBT theory and practice. In Chapter 5 I discussed the therapist's work in eliciting client's goals that are realistic, achievable and serve as a beacon for the work that both client and therapist need to do to help the client achieve these goals. However, that is not to deny that REB therapists need to draw on a range of technical skills. The technical side of REBT will be the main focus of this concluding chapter, which considers tasks from a working alliance perspective. In particular, I will first discuss the more technical aspects of the therapist's tasks and how the therapist helps the client to gain the most from their tasks so that they can make the most out of REBT. I will then consider tasks in REBT from the client's perspective.

Therapist tasks

In the first main section of this chapter, I will list important therapist tasks that help the client to achieve their goals and will discuss how their implementation is guided by the working alliance perspective.

Assessing the client's problems

It is essential that the REB therapist helps themselves and their client to understand the client's problems and that the therapist does this with reference to the *ABC* framework (see Chapter 1). From the perspective of the working alliance, the therapist needs to ensure that their client understands the *ABC* framework and how it is relevant to understanding their problems.

Assessing the client's meta-disturbance

According to REBT theory, clients frequently disturb themselves about their disturbance. Furthermore, this 'meta-disturbance' can sometimes be more problematic for clients than the problem for which they are seeking help. Before the REB therapist assesses for the presence and nature of a meta-disturbance problem, they need to give the client a rationale for doing so, and should only proceed once the client has indicated that they understand this rationale.

Discovering the client's goals

Having assessed the client's designated problem, the REB therapist needs to ascertain the client's goals in relation to this problem. As discussed in Chapter 5, the most important consideration at this stage is for the therapist and client to agree on the client's goals.

Helping the client to examine their rigid and extreme attitudes and flexible and non-extreme attitudes

REBT is fundamentally concerned with facilitating changes in attitudes. This requires the REB therapist to carry out some rather specialised tasks that help and encourage the client to:

* understand the role that their attitudes play in their problems and in the solutions to their problems
* identify their relevant rigid and extreme attitudes towards the adversity at *A* that underpin their problems, and alternative relevant flexible and non-extreme attitudes that underpin the solution to their problems
* stand back to examine both sets of attitudes to determine the empirical, logical and pragmatic status of these attitudes
* commit themself to strengthening their flexible and non-extreme attitudes.

Prior to carrying out the above tasks, it is important that the REB therapist provides the client with a rationale for the process of examining attitudes, and that the client fully understands and consents to taking part in such a process.

Negotiating and reviewing homework assignments with the client

Negotiating and reviewing clients' homework assignments is one of the REB therapist's key tasks. The purpose of such tasks is to help the client to make the most of what they do *between* sessions as this is, in some ways, more important than what they do *during* their therapy sessions. Just as homework is a negotiated process, it is essential that the client is fully involved in this process. With this in mind, the REB therapist will help the client to understand the importance of homework in REBT, will answer any questions the client might have about homework and will obtain the client's commitment to engage in the process of negotiating, executing and reviewing homework.

Negotiating homework assignments

When the REB therapist negotiates a homework assignment with the client, the therapist needs to:

- allow themself sufficient time to negotiate the assignment at the end of the therapy session
- ensure that the assignment follows logically from the work in the session
- ensure, whenever possible, that the assignment allows the client to rehearse a flexible and/or non-extreme attitude while acting and thinking in ways that are consistent with that attitude
- ensure that the client understands the purpose of carrying out the negotiated assignment and how doing so will help them to achieve their goals
- ensure that the client has the skills and ability to carry out the assignment
- elicit a commitment from the client to carry out the homework assignment rather than to 'try' to do it
- encourage the client to specify when and where they will carry out the assignment
- help the client to identify and deal with obstacles to homework completion
- help the client to identify behaviours that are designed to keep them safe in their mind while they are carrying out the assignment and encourage them to refrain from using these safety-seeking strategies

- rehearse the homework assignment with the client in the therapy session in either role-play or imagery
- encourage the client to make a written note of the homework assignment, its purpose and where and when they are going to do it.

Reviewing homework assignments

The REB therapist needs to ensure that they review the client's homework. Otherwise, the client will get the impression that homework assignments are not important. When reviewing a homework assignment with the client, the REB therapist needs to:

- check whether the client has done all of the homework assignment and if they did not complete it – either in part or in full – explore their reasons for not doing so
- explore the reasons why the client made any modifications to the homework assignment and then address these reasons
- check what the client learned from doing the assignment, assuming that they did it in full
- help the client to capitalise on their success in doing the assignment
- help the client to deal constructively with any failures encountered in doing the assignment
- correct any errors or misconceptions that the client expresses during the process of reviewing their homework.

Helping the client to generalise their gains

Once the client has made progress on their nominated problem, the REB therapist offers to help them to generalise their gains to other problems that they have and wish to deal with in therapy. If the client wishes to do this, the therapist helps the client to:

- generalise gains from one specific example of their problem to other examples of the problem where the adversity is the same
- generalise their gains from one problem to another problem where the adversity is different
- identify and examine their general flexible and non-extreme attitudes
- rehearse and act in ways that are consistent with specific examples of their general flexible and non-extreme attitudes in relevant situations.

Helping the client to identify and examine their doubts, reservations and objections (DROs)

As I have hopefully demonstrated throughout this book, during the course of therapy the REB therapist is careful to explain to the client the ideas and practices associated with REBT. It is also important to note that a number of these ideas are counter-intuitive, and that the client may have doubts, reservations and objections (DROs) towards some of them (Dryden, 2001; 2022). For example, the client may have DROs about:

*   giving up rigid/extreme attitudes in favour of flexible/non-extreme attitudes
*   moving away from unhealthy negative emotions (UNEs) in favour of healthy negative emotions (HNEs)
*   acting in ways deemed constructive by REBT theory rather than acting in ways considered unconstructive by the theory.

Responding to a client's doubts, reservations and objections

If the REB therapist suspects that the client may be holding a DRO, then they will do the following:

*   Mention the possibility that the client may have a DRO and invite the client to comment on this.
*   If the client agrees that they have a DRO, then the therapist invites the client to elaborate and conveys empathy with the client's position.
*   Make a mental note of the problem with the client's DRO.
*   Invite the client to hear their view of the client's DRO.
*   If the client accepts the invitation, the therapist expresses their view. If the client does not accept the invitation, the therapist refers this to the reflection process for discussion.
*   Engage the client in a discussion about the DRO until it is adequately addressed.

Helping the client to prevent relapse

A relapse can be defined as going back to square one after the client has achieved the changes they were seeking. Relapse prevention is therefore another important task for the REB therapist. However, before commencing such work with a client, it is important the therapist ensures that the client wants to participate in a relapse prevention process. This involves the therapist explaining the importance of relapse prevention, and what such preventative work entails. If the client is then interested in working with their therapist to prevent relapse, the therapist should help them as follows.

Identifying and dealing with the client's vulnerability factors

What I mean by vulnerability factors is factors to which the client is susceptible and which, if not dealt with, will result in the client returning to their problem state. The REB therapist should encourage the client to identify and deal with these factors one at a time.

Encourage the client to take the lead in assessing the vulnerability factor. Given that the client has made some desired changes by this stage in their therapy, they should have developed some REBT skills in assessing their problems. Therefore, they should be encouraged, with the therapist's help, to take the lead in assessing each of their vulnerability factors using REBT's *ABC* framework.

Encourage the client to deal with the variables that account for the existence of each vulnerability factor. This usually involves the client developing a set of flexible and/or non-extreme attitudes towards the adversity that features in their vulnerability factor and a set of accompanying behaviours that rest on these attitudes that they can implement at appropriate times.

Encourage the client to rehearse dealing with the vulnerability factor in imagery. Before the client seeks out the vulnerability factor in real life, it is helpful for the therapist to encourage them to rehearse ways of dealing with the factor using imagery (or imagination). In this respect, it is preferable for the REB therapist to encourage the client to use *coping* imagery (where they initially struggle in the face of the vulnerability factor but succeed in the end) as opposed to *mastery* imagery (where they succeed at the outset).

Encourage the client to deal with the vulnerability factor in real life. When the REB therapist encourages the client to deal with their vulnerability factor in real life, they encourage the client to go at their own pace in facing the adversity that features in the vulnerability factor. However, the therapist also guards against the client being guided by avoidance of discomfort, and may therefore invite the client to consider the 'challenging, but not overwhelming' principle (Dryden, 1985). This involves discouraging the client from facing the featured adversity too gradually, and encouraging them alternatively to face this adversity when it is challenging for them to do so, but not to the extent that they are likely to feel overwhelmed by the experience.

Dealing with client lapses

When a client has a lapse, this can be viewed as a minor and usually temporary return to a problem state. The REB therapist is advised to help a client to deal with lapses in the following ways.

Help the client to deal with their disturbance about lapsing

Some clients hold an attitude along the lines of 'I must not have a lapse'. If such clients have a lapse, they are likely to be disturbed about this and to conclude that they have 'blown' their chances of benefiting from therapy. The REB therapist can help such clients to recognise that the most effective way forward is for them to develop a healthier attitude towards lapsing. If the client agrees, then the therapist will help them with this.

Help the client to learn from lapsing

A client who is not disturbed about lapsing is more likely to learn from a lapse than a client who finds this disturbing. A non-disturbed frame of mind helps the client to stand back and understand and deal with the factors that explained their lapse, so that future lapses are less likely, or less significant.

Help the client to see that lapsing is common and encourage them to renew their commitment to change

The REB therapist will advise the client that it is quite common for a person to lapse when participating in any change programme. This is sometimes referred to as 'normalising' lapsing. If the client then goes on to have a lapse, they can recognise this as a 'normal' part of the change process. This can help the client to resume and renew their commitment to deal with their problem and work towards their goal.

Dealing with client relapses

Even if a client has made significant efforts to deal with their vulnerability factors and any lapses they have experienced, they may continue to disturb themself about the prospect of having a relapse. If the client then *does* have a relapse, this is something they will additionally have to deal with.

Before assisting the client with a relapse, it is important that the REB therapist gives the client a rationale for doing so and that the client consents to receiving such assistance.

Help the client deal with their disturbance about relapse

When a client disturbs themself about relapsing, they do this either before or after the relapse has occurred.

Treating relapse as an *A*. Irrespective of *when* the client has disturbed themself about relapsing, the REB therapist helps the client to use the *ABC* framework (with relapse placed at *A*) to deal with this. The therapist then helps the client to carry out a relevant problem assessment and to develop a set of flexible and non-extreme attitudes towards relapsing, whether they have relapsed or not.

Treating relapse as a cognitive C

A client may sometimes overestimate the possibility that they will have a relapse. When this happens, it is due to the client holding rigid and extreme attitudes towards relapse (as discussed above) and/or the client disturbing themself about a less negative adversity (e.g. lapsing) and going on to create a distorted cognitive *C* (e.g. 'I will relapse'). In the latter case, the REB therapist can help the client to identify how they created this distorted cognitive *C* and then to change this to a more realistic *C* that is based on a healthier approach to dealing with the less negative adversity.

Help the client to learn from relapse

When the REB therapist has helped the client to un-disturb themself about relapsing, the client can learn from relapse if they *do* relapse, or even if they do *not* relapse. The therapist can facilitate such learning by asking the client questions such as 'If you *were* to have a relapse, what would have had to happen for that to occur?' By learning from actual or imagined relapse, the client is helped to take the horror (but not the badness) out of relapse and to develop the skills to prevent a relapse from happening, or from happening again. The client can also recognise that if they do relapse, they can then choose between staying in their relapsed state or renewing their commitment to change.

Helping the client to become their own REB therapist

The REB therapist's ultimate or ideal goal is probably to help the client to internalise REBT skills so that they can use such skills for themself and thus become their own therapist. However, not all clients want to stay in therapy to become their own therapist, so the REB therapist will only carry out tasks in this area with the client's agreement. When the client indicates that they *do* wish to be helped to become their own therapist, the therapist assists them by using a prompting style of inter-action. As discussed in Chapter 3, this involves the therapist gradually handing over control to the client for the running of sessions, while also prompting them when this is required.

Ending therapy

The REB therapist's final task concerns concluding therapy with the client. From the perspective of working alliance theory, it is particularly important that the therapist and client agree on the best way to conclude their work together. From an REBT perspective, the REB therapist will also consider the ending of therapy with respect to the following:

*   gradually increasing the gap between sessions, when the therapist and client agree that the client is ready to do so
*   setting/planning a time for the client to end therapy (with the understanding that the door is open should they want to return), when the therapist and client agree that the client has reached a stage where it is appropriate for them to discuss such a time
*   helping the client to review (towards the end of therapy) what they have achieved and learned from their therapy journey
*   allowing the client to raise and discuss any unfinished business
*   giving the client an opportunity to express and work through any issues they might have regarding ending therapy and dealing with life without therapy and the therapist; it is here that mutual feelings of sadness and appreciation are generally expressed
*   agreeing with the client the types of situations in which it would be appropriate for the client to contact the therapist in the future (these would normally be situations where the client has made a determined, but unsuccessful, effort to help themself, or where the client feels they do not have sufficient coping resources to deal with a new problem)
*   planning a future review session to monitor the client's progress.

Therapist skill

There has been some research that suggests that the therapist's skill in performing their therapeutic tasks has a positive influence on client outcome (e.g. Luborsky et al., 1985). When such research is considered from a working alliance perspective, it similarly suggests that the extent to which a client makes progress in therapy may be associated with their therapist's level of skill in performing their tasks.

By implication, we cannot automatically assume that well-trained REB therapists are equally skilled at performing their tasks. Similarly, skill factors need to be emphasised in therapist training and supervision – perhaps more so than has previously been the case. This could involve trainers and supervisors placing less reliance on trainees' and practitioners' descriptions of what they did in therapy sessions, and requiring more in the way of objective and detailed evidence (such as digital video or sound recordings) that can be used to appraise their skills more specifically.

Client tasks

Further to the above considerations about the REB therapist's tasks, it is important to emphasise that the client also has responsibilities in the working alliance process. If the client does not exercise their responsibility for self-change, they will not change. Therefore it is important that both the therapist *and* the client carry out their respective tasks. With this in mind, I will continue this chapter by providing an outline of the REBT client's tasks:

* honestly disclosing their problems
* being open to the REBT framework and giving their informed consent to proceed
* disclosing any doubts, reservations and objections that they may have about REB theory and practice
* engaging with a range of in-session and between-session tasks; such tasks include:
  * applying the *ABC* framework to assess examples of their problem(s)
  * examining their rigid/extreme and flexible/non-extreme attitudes
  * utilising a range of methods to weaken conviction in the former and strengthen conviction in the latter
  * implementing agreed and negotiated homework tasks
* putting into practice what they learn in therapy outside therapy
* taking responsibility for applying REBT self-change skills after therapy, if relevant.

Client tasks in the context of the REBT working alliance – what the therapist needs to do

The REB therapist's approach to helping their client with their tasks can be informed by working alliance theory in several ways.

The therapist needs to help the client to understand the nature of their therapeutic tasks

When a client is in psychoanalysis, they are invited to lie down on a couch and to speak freely about anything that comes to mind, without searching for a specific subject or topic. This invitation implicitly specifies the nature of the client's task in this approach to therapy. In many other approaches to therapy the client is expected to tell the therapist about the problems that they have been grappling with, while in solution-focused therapy the client is helped to minimise 'problem talk' and instead to engage in 'solution talk'. Aware of how important it is for clients to understand their role in the therapy process and more specifically what their tasks are in that process, some therapists formally attempt to initiate clients into their role at the outset. However, most of the time the client learns what their tasks are implicitly. There are a number of resources that have been designed to teach clients explicitly in REBT what tasks they have to perform (see Dryden, 2001; 2022, for an example).

If the client does not either explicitly or implicitly understand that they have tasks to perform in the REBT process and what these tasks are, and if the client has also not agreed to these tasks, then this may well constitute a potential obstacle to the client's progress in therapy. Therefore, it is the therapist's task to help the client to understand their tasks. Even when the therapist has attempted to do this, it may later come to light that the client has forgotten or misunderstood their tasks. As with other potential obstacles, this may be dealt with by referring the matter for discussion to that part of the therapy dialogue that I call the reflection process, where therapist and client step back and discuss what has gone on between them during therapy sessions.

The therapist needs to help the client to understand the instrumental value of their tasks in REBT

As noted earlier, tasks are best conceptualised as ways of achieving therapeutic goals. However, even when a client understands the nature of the tasks they are required to carry out in REBT, they may not always see the instrumental value of carrying out these tasks (i.e. with respect to achieving their outcome goals). For example, a client may not see how examining their rigid and extreme attitudes towards competence will necessarily help them to overcome their problem of examination anxiety. Therefore, from a working alliance perspective, it is vital that the REB therapist helps the client to understand the link between carrying out their therapeutic tasks and achieving their outcome goals. This point applies to tasks that the client performs *within* their therapy sessions as well as tasks they perform *between* therapy sessions in their daily life.

*The therapist needs to ensure that the client has the ability
to execute their tasks in REBT*

The execution of certain tasks can facilitate client change in REBT. However, it is important that the client is set tasks that are within their level of ability. If the client is unable to carry out their therapeutic tasks, this can pose a threat to the working alliance. Therefore, the REB therapist takes care to choose tasks that are within their client's level of ability.

*The therapist should ensure that the client has skills to execute their
tasks in REBT*

Even if a client has the ability to execute a therapeutic task, they may not possess the skills to do so. In such instances, the REB therapist needs to train the client in the required skills before asking them to execute the task. As noted earlier, there are several REBT books (e.g. Dryden, 2001; 2022) that can serve as a resource for therapists who wish to help their clients to acquire such skills.

*The therapist needs to encourage the client to develop a reasonable
degree of confidence to execute their tasks in REBT*

There are some client tasks (particularly those associated with between-session 'homework assignments') that require a certain level of task confidence if they are to be performed successfully. Therefore, even if a client understands the nature of the task, can see its therapeutic relevance, and has the ability and the skills to carry it out, it is important for the REB therapist to additionally consider whether the client has sufficient confidence to execute that task.

When the client lacks such confidence, the REB therapist can assist them in two ways. The first of these involves helping the client to practise the task in controlled and 'safe' conditions (usually within the therapy session) until they feel sufficiently confident to execute the task on their own. The second involves pointing out that it is rare to feel confident before a first attempt at an activity, as confidence is usually gained by undertaking (i.e. practising) an activity. On this basis, the therapist encourages the client to carry out the task unconfidently.

*The therapist needs to ensure that client tasks in REBT should be
sufficiently potent*

The therapist is responsible for ensuring that the client's tasks have sufficient therapeutic potency to facilitate the achievement of their goals.

In this respect, it is best to consider the use of cognitive restructuring techniques in REBT as preparation for later action-based changes of beliefs. This is because cognitive techniques may have limited potency on their own (Emmelkamp, Kuipers & Eggeraat, 1978), and the most potent client tasks in REBT are likely to be behavioural tasks, albeit when these tasks are also founded on flexible and non-extreme attitudes.

The therapist should help the client understand their therapist's tasks

I previously noted (in this section concerning how the REB therapist should help the client with their tasks) that the therapist needs to help the client to understand the tasks that are expected of them in their REBT. From a working alliance perspective, it is also important that the REB therapist assumes responsibility for helping the client to understand the nature of the tasks that they (i.e. the therapist) will carry out to support the client, the rationale for intervening in particular ways, and the way in which the therapist's tasks relate to the client's tasks. The explicit nature of REBT lends itself to such explicit communication.

The more the client can understand how their tasks relate to their therapist's tasks, the more the client and therapist can focus on effective execution of their respective tasks with respect to their main aim (as emphasised above) of facilitating the client's attainment of their goals. If the client does not understand the nature of their therapist's tasks and how their therapist's tasks relate to their own tasks, the client can become distracted from their tasks and start questioning what the therapist is doing and the therapist's competence to help them. If these client doubts are not explored and addressed in the reflection process, they pose a threat to all aspects of the working alliance.

The four domains of the working alliance are interrelated

In this chapter I have focused on tasks as if they are a separate domain of the working alliance in REBT. I have similarly dealt with bonds, views and goals in separate previous chapters. However, as noted at the end of Chapter 2, it is important to remember that, in reality, these four working alliance domains are interrelated, and I would like to conclude this chapter, and indeed this book, by illustrating the dynamic and interactive nature of the four working alliance domains. When the therapist's and client's tasks are structured effectively, this can help to clarify the client's goals and to strengthen the initial (and ongoing) bond between the therapist and client.

- When the therapist responds promptly and effectively to any indications that the client lacks trust in the therapeutic relationship, this can help the client to engage more fully with the REBT change process and to concentrate on executing their tasks. This also helps to strengthen the bond between the therapist and the client.
- When the therapist handles a client's 'reluctance' sensitively and effectively, this helps the 'reluctant' client to commit themself to the therapy process and to set goals that are in their own best interest (as opposed to setting goals that significant others might have for them).
- When the therapist selects tasks that lend themselves to the client's particular life/work style, this helps the client to appreciate that their therapist understands them, and also serves to strengthen the task domain of the working alliance.
- When the therapist is able to provide the client with early reassurance that they can satisfy the client's expectations for therapy, this helps to establish a solid relationship (bond) which will encourage the client to take on appropriate challenges (tasks) that facilitate client change at subsequent stages of their work together.
- When the therapist becomes aware of so-called 'transference' phenomena, and is also able to handle these sensitively, this helps to prevent the development of self- and relationship-defeating ways of thinking and behaving during therapy. It similarly helps the client to achieve their goals.
- When the therapist is skilled at handling the termination of therapy and a client's possible attempts to terminate therapy prematurely, this helps to consolidate the client's progress towards their goal and to bring the bond between therapist and client to a mutually satisfying end.

This brings me to the end of the book. I hope you have found it valuable. If you have any feedback to offer me, please send it to my email address: windy@windydryden.com

References

Barker, C., Pistrang, N., Shapiro, D.A., & Shaw, I. (1990). Coping and help-seeking in the UK adult population. *British Journal of Clinical Psychology*, *29*, 271–285.

Beck, A.T., Rush, A.J., Shaw, B.F., & Emery, G. (1979). *Cognitive therapy of depression*. New York: Guilford.

Bordin, E.S. (1979). The generalizability of the psychoanalytic concept of the working alliance. *Psychotherapy: Theory, Research and Practice, 16(3)*, 252–260.

DiGiuseppe, R., Leaf, R., & Linscott, J. (1993). The therapeutic relationship in rational-emotive therapy: Some preliminary data. *Journal of Rational-Emotive and Cognitive-Behavior Therapy*, *11*, 223–233.

Dorn, F.J. (Ed.) (1984). *The social influence process in counseling and psychotherapy*. Springfield, IL: Charles C. Thomas.

Dryden, W. (1985). Challenging, but not overwhelming: A compromise in negotiating homework assignments. *British Journal of Cognitive Psychotherapy*, *3(1)*, 77–80.

Dryden, W. (1989). The therapeutic alliance as an integrating framework. In W. Dryden (Ed.), *Key issues for counselling in action* (pp. 1–15). London: Sage.

Dryden, W. (2001). *Reason to change: A rational emotive behaviour therapy (REBT) workbook*. Hove, East Sussex: Brunner-Routledge.

Dryden, W. (2006). *Counselling in a nutshell*. London: Sage.

Dryden, W. (2011). *Counselling in a nutshell. 2nd edition*. London: Sage.

Dryden, W. (2022). *Reason to change: A rational emotive behaviour therapy workbook. 2nd edition*. Abingdon, Oxon: Routledge.

Ellis, A. (1959). Requisite conditions for basic personality change. *Journal of Consulting Psychology*, *23*, 538–540.

Ellis, A. (1963). Toward a more precise definition of 'emotional' and 'intellectual' insight. *Psychological Reports*, *13*, 125–126.

Ellis, A. (2002). *Overcoming resistance: A rational emotive behavior therapy integrated approach. 2nd edition*. New York: Springer.

Ellis, A., & Dryden, W. (1985). Dilemmas in giving warmth or love to clients: An interview with Albert Ellis. In W. Dryden, *Therapists' dilemmas* (pp. 5–16). London: Harper & Row.

Emmelkamp, P.M.G., Kuipers, A.C.M., & Eggeraat, J.B. (1978). Cognitive modification versus prolonged exposure in vivo: A comparison with agoraphobics as subjects. *Behaviour Research and Therapy*, *16*, 33–41.

Grieger, R., & Boyd, J. (1980). *Rational-emotive therapy: A skills-based approach.* New York: Van Nostrand Reinhold.

Jacobs, M. (2017). *Psychodynamic counselling in action. 5th edition.* London: Sage.

Lazarus, A.A. (1989). *The practice of multimodal therapy.* Baltimore, MD: Johns Hopkins University Press.

Leahy, R.L. (2007). Schematic mismatch in the therapeutic relationship: A social-cognitive model. In P. Gilbert & R.L. Leahy (Eds.), *The therapeutic relationship in the cognitive behavioral psychotherapies* (pp. 229–254). London: Routledge/Taylor & Francis Group.

Luborsky, L., McLellan, A.T., Woody, G.E., O'Brien, C.P., & Auerbach, A. (1985). Therapist success and its determinants. *Archives of General Psychiatry*, *42*, 602–611.

Mahrer, A. (Ed.). (1967). *The goals of psychotherapy.* Englewood Cliffs, NJ: Prentice-Hall.

Miranda, R., & Andersen, S.M. (2007). The therapeutic relationship: Implications from social cognition and transference. In P. Gilbert & R.L. Leahy (Eds.), *The therapeutic relationship in the cognitive behavioral psychotherapies* (pp. 63–89). London: Routledge/Taylor & Francis Group.

Pistrang, N., & Barker, C. (1992). Clients' beliefs about psychological problems. *Counselling Psychology Quarterly*, *5*, 325–336.

Rogers, C.R. (1957). The necessary and sufficient conditions of therapeutic personality change. *Journal of Consulting Psychology*, *21*, 95–103.

Seabury, B., Seabury, B., & Garvin, C. (2011). *Foundations of interpersonal practice in social work: Promoting competence in generalist practice.* Thousand Oaks, CA: Sage Publications.

Walen, S.R., DiGiuseppe, R., & Dryden, W. (1992). *A practitioner's guide to rational-emotive therapy. 2nd edition.* New York: Oxford University Press.

Wessler, R.A., & Wessler, R.L. (1980). *The principles and practice of rational-emotive therapy.* San Francisco, CA: Jossey-Bass.

Woods, P.J. (1991). Orthodox RET taught effectively with graphics, feedback on irrational beliefs, a structured homework series, and models of disputation. In M.E. Bernard (Ed.), *Using rational-emotive therapy effectively: A practitioner's guide* (pp. 69–109). New York: Plenum.

Index

For Product Safety Concerns and Information please contact our EU
representative GPSR@taylorandfrancis.com
Taylor & Francis Verlag GmbH, Kaufingerstraße 24, 80331 München, Germany